bath &
beauty

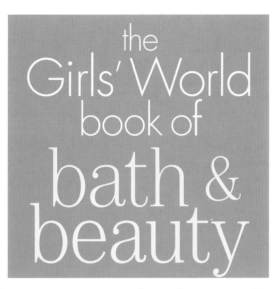

the
# Girls' World
## book of
# bath &
# beauty

## fresh ideas & fun recipes for hair, skin, nails & more

## Allison Chandler Smith

# LARK BOOKS

A Division of Sterling Publishing Co., Inc.
New York

Editor: Joanne O'Sullivan
Art Director: Dana Irwin
Photographer: Sandra Stambaugh
Cover Designer: Barbara Zaretsky
Illustrator: Orrin Lundgren
Production Assistance: Lance Wille,
Shannon Yokeley
Editorial Assistance: Delores Gosnell

Library of Congress Cataloging-in-Publication Data

Smith, Allison Chandler, 1966-
  The girl's world book of bath & beauty : fresh & fun ideas for hair,
skin, nails & more / by Allison Chandler Smith.
      p. cm.
Includes index.

  ISBN 1-57990-492-0
1.  Cosmetics--Juvenile literature. 2.  Soap--Juvenile literature. [1.
Cosmetics. 2. Soap. 3. Handicraft.]  I. Title.
  TP983.S65 2004
  668'.55--dc22

                                                      2003014137


10 9 8 7 6 5 4 3


Published by Lark Books, a division of
Sterling Publishing Co., Inc.
387 Park Avenue South, New York, N.Y. 10016

© 2004, Allison Chandler Smith

Distributed in Canada by Sterling Publishing,
c/o Canadian Manda Group, 165 Dufferin Street
Toronto, Ontario, Canada M6K 3H6

Distributed in the U.K. by Guild of Master Craftsman Publications Ltd.,
Castle Place, 166 High Street, Lewes, East Sussex, England
BN7 1XU
Tel: (+ 44) 1273 477374, Fax: (+ 44) 1273 478606,
Email: pubs@thegmcgroup.com, Web: www.gmcpublications.com

Distributed in Australia by Capricorn Link (Australia) Pty Ltd.,
P.O. Box 704, Windsor, NSW 2756 Australia

The written instructions, photographs, designs, patterns, and projects in this volume
are intended for the personal use of the reader and may be reproduced for that pur-
pose only. Any other use, especially commercial use, is forbidden under law without
written permission of the copyright holder.

Every effort has been made to ensure that all the information in this book is accu-
rate. However, due to differing conditions, tools, and individual skills, the publisher
cannot be responsible for any injuries, losses, and other damages that may result
from the use of the information in this book.

If you have questions or comments about this book, please contact:
Lark Books
67 Broadway
Asheville, NC 28801
(828) 253-0467

Manufactured in China

ISBN 1-57990-492-0

For information about custom editions, special sales, premium and
corporate purchases, please contact Sterling Special Sales Department
at 800-805-5489 or specialsales@sterlingpub.com

Dedication

For my husband, Tama, and my daughters, Kerewin, Devon, Shakara, and Indica, my
true sources of unconditional love and inspiration.

# Contents

# Introduction

There are certain things a girl should not attempt to make at home. Make your own fireworks? I wouldn't recommend it. Design and fill out your own report card? Not such a good idea. But make your own bath and beauty products? Go for it!

As you walk down the aisle of your local drugstore looking at all the lotions, shampoos, bath oils, and perfumes, they all look and smell so wonderful that it may seem impossible to recreate them yourself. Plus, how are you going to find all those strange ingredients like isobuytlparaben or sodium laurel sulfate when you can't even pronounce them?

Well, here's some good news. You don't need chemicals or a lab coat to make fantastic moisturizers, bath salts, scrubs, lip glosses, or shampoos. You can make them with natural ingredients from health food stores and other supplies that are easy to find, too. The *even better* news is that it's fun to make them on your own or with friends. All you need are some great recipes and your own creativity. This book supplies the recipes (and a whole lot more)—just use your imagination and you're on your way.

You already know that it's important to take care of your skin, hair, and body to keep them in top shape. But you don't have to spend all your money on expensive products in order to look and feel your best. Making your own products is a great way to do something nice for yourself or your friends. You know what's in the product, so you know it's good for you. Plus, you can customize the colors and fragrance so you get a perfume, shampoo, or soap that's really *you*. Better still, you can make your friend, mother, or sister a gift that's really *her*.

The Getting Started section of the book introduces you to all the supplies and ingredients you'll need to make the projects and tells you where to find them. There's a useful guide to essential oils and fragrances, and a section on embellishing your product containers and creating your own line of spa products.

Chapter 1 focuses on the skin you're in. You'll find recipes for lotions, scrubs, washes, masks, and toners. This chapter is also full of helpful information on skin types and breakouts and how to deal with them, as well as good ideas for daily skin care routines.

Skin                    Hair                    Bath

In Chapter 2, it's all about hair. Make shampoos, hair accessories, and a special hot oil treatment that leaves your hair smooth and shiny. You'll learn to identify your hair type and discover super tips for keeping your hair looking its best.

Chapter 3 is good clean fun. From soaps to bath bombs, salts, and jam, you'll find recipes for special bath products that are fun to make and that smell fantastic.

In Chapter 4 there are cool body care projects, like making lip balm, lip gloss, and powder. Plus you'll find interesting information on scents and smells you like (perfume and shower sprays), and those you don't like (body odor and bath breath), and lots of neat tips and advice.

Your hands and feet take center stage in Chapter 5. You'll learn manicure and pedicure basics and find recipes for tons of cool products, from cooling foot spray to hand cream. If you're a little adventurous, try applying a mendhi henna tattoo or use gel pens to create temporary designs on your hands, arms, or wherever. You can even learn to make toe rings to dress up your feet for summer.

Finally, in Chapter 6, try focusing on your mind and spirit. There are instructions for making a relaxing eye pillow and a teddy bear filled with lavender to help soothe your aching muscles. Make a Zen sand garden and watch your stress melt away. You'll also learn relaxation techniques and find out about some interesting rites of passage for girls from different cultures.

I hope you'll enjoy making these recipes as much as I did. Once you've got the hang of working with the materials, you'll be able to make them in no time, and maybe even create some new ones of your own. So give it a try. You'll have a great time making something special for a friend, or best of all, just pampering yourself—you deserve it!

# Getting Started

You don't need to get straight A's in science to make your own beauty products, and you don't need to spend all your savings on equipment or turn your kitchen into a laboratory. In fact, you probably already have a lot of what you need in your house.

The following list includes almost *everything* you need to make *every* project in the book. Since you probably don't want to do every single one (at least not all at once), don't worry if you don't have some of the supplies. Start slow—take it project by project. Eventually you'll have a great stash of tools and ingredients to work with.

## Supplies

There's nothing too complicated or unusual about most of what you'll need to make the projects in the book. If you don't already have this stuff, you can buy it at a drugstore, craft store, or kitchen store.

Flour sifter

Glass measuring cup

Measuring spoons

Spoons

Cheese grater

Cookie sheet

Plastic pitcher

Soap molds (if you want to make soap)

Craft sticks

Hot glue gun and glue sticks

Eyedropper

Small-and medium-sized mixing bowls

Zip-top plastic sandwich bags in different sizes

Cellophane wrap

Small funnel

Toothpicks

Cotton balls

Cotton swabs

Wax paper

Pot holders

Coffee filters

Mortar and pestle (these can be handy, but they're not a necessity)

Small glass and metal decorative containers

Small collection of ribbons, strings, fabric, stickers, buttons, and other out-of-the-ordinary items for adorning your containers

Ruler or measuring tape

Felt markers and pencils

Straight pins

Scissors

Labels in a variety of shapes and sizes

Microwave

Blender or hand mixer

Food processor

Pots and pans

# Beauty Product Ingredients

Getting the ingredients you need to make the products isn't quite as simple as finding all the tools and supplies, but don't worry—you won't need to go out and find any 25-letter-long ingredients. Remember, these are *natural* beauty products. You may never have noticed them before, but you can usually find all the ingredients you'll need at your local drugstore, grocery store, craft store, or health food store. Like the tools and supplies, you don't need to buy all the ingredients on the list. Try the recipes one at a time, and find out which ones you like best. You'll only need to buy the ingredients that you need for those projects, and you'll probably have some left over to make other projects that use the same stuff. After a while you'll have a great stock of ingredients to draw from.

Since you may never have heard of some of these ingredients before, read the guide on pages 12 and 13 to discover the special properties of different items. Next to each item you'll see a symbol to tell you where you can find the ingredient (see key on page 13). Once you work with the recipes and become more comfortable with how the different ingredients work together to make finished products, you may want to branch out and create special recipes of your own. For recipes that require the use of a blender or stove, you'll need to have an adult present when making the product. You'll see the "parental supervision" icon next to the instructions to remind you.

# Ingredients List

**ALOE VERA GEL.** A gel made from the leaves of the aloe vera plant. It contains lots of vitamins, and it's great for healing dry, itchy skin.

**BAKING SODA.** A powder that's often used in baking, just like the name says. It's also a natural deodorizer, and when combined with certain other ingredients, it fizzes!

**BEESWAX.** Comes from a honeycomb after the honey is removed. It's hard at room temperature and is used to thicken creams and lotions. Because it's water resistant, it's also really great for protecting dry, chapped skin.

**BENTONITE CLAY POWDER.** Clay from the southwestern United States. It's used for drying out oily skin.

**BORAX.** An emulsifying (see page 15) powder used in many recipes. It contains a chemical often used to emulsify a water-based liquid with an oil-based liquid (see box on page 14). Don't put it directly on your skin, eat it, or inhale it, as it can irritate your skin and is not meant to be taken internally.

**CITRIC ACID.** An acid that exists naturally in fruit. It's used as a preservative to keep your creams and lotions from losing their color and texture, or as a flavoring. When combined with other ingredients, it fizzes, so it's great in bath bombs or scrubbing salts. Citric acid is a natural alpha-hydroxy, which means it helps adjust the pH balance (acid content) of your products and leaves your skin feeling smooth.

**CITRUS PEELS.** The preserved peels of citrus fruit, such as oranges or lemons.

**COCOA BUTTER.** The fat from the seeds of the cocoa plant. It's used as a moisturizer. It's solid at room temperature, but it softens quickly at body temperature.

**COCONUT OIL.** The oil of the coconut, it's used for cooking as well as in beauty products. It's usually solid at room temperature. A very rich, emollient (see page 15), it's used in a wide variety of beauty products. It smells faintly of coconuts.

**CORNSTARCH.** A fine powder made from corn. It's used to thicken and bind your lotions and creams so they aren't too watery. It's also very absorbent so it's often used as a drying agent instead of powder.

**COSMETIC-GRADE GLITTER.** Used to add a fun sparkle to soaps, body gels, and lotions.

**DISTILLED WATER.** Water that has been purified through a process of boiling and condensation.

**EPSOM SALTS.** Used in baths to relax muscles. These salts can be dehydrating, so you should drink a glass of water before you use them in your tub.

**GLYCERIN.** A thick, colorless, and odorless liquid that comes from vegetables. It helps lotions and creams keep their moisture and emollience (see page 15).

**GRAPESEED OIL.** Very light and easily absorbed oil. It's odorless, so it's great for mixing with essential oils.

**LANOLIN.** A substance that comes from sheep's wool. It's used as an emulsifier (see page 15). Lanolin is very rich, and it creates a moisture barrier to protect chapped skin.

**LOOFA.** A sponge that comes from the inside of a dried-out gourd. It has dense fibers that make it great for exfoliating skin that's prone to breakouts (just don't use it on your face).

**MORTAR AND PESTLE.** A stone or wooden bowl and blunt tool used for grinding dried herbs (see photo on page 11).

**ORANGE WATER.** A sweet-smelling liquid made in a process similar to making tea. Orange peels are placed in hot water to steep. The orange peels are removed from the water and then the water can be used for cosmetics.

**PUMICE.** Powdered volcanic rock that's very abrasive. It's used on hands and feet to remove rough spots.

**ROSE WATER.** Made in the same manner as orange water (see Orange Water), but rose petals are used instead.

**RUBBING ALCOHOL.** Antiseptic and astringent (see page 15 for definitions), it also has a preservative effect.

**SEA SALT.** The salt that's left over after seawater evaporates. It's used a lot in baths.

**SHEA BUTTER.** A smooth, rich butter made from the nut of the Karite tree in Africa.

**SOAP COLORS.** Strong water-based dyes that can be used for coloring soaps, creams, lotions, toners, etc. You can use most powdered soap colors in lip balm and lip gloss recipes. The exceptions are the blue and green soap colors, which contain ingredients that you don't want to put near your mouth.

**SWEET ALMOND OIL.** A light, good-quality oil that's relatively inexpensive and is used in many recipes. It's made from the oil of almonds.

**TEA TREE OIL.** An essential oil that comes from the tea tree in Australia and New Zealand. It's naturally deodorizing and antiseptic (see page 15). It's often used on rashes and other skin problems.

**VITAMIN E.** An antioxidant that naturally occurs in vegetable oils, some grains, and eggs. It's very nourishing for the skin, and also prevents oils from going bad.

**WITCH HAZEL.** A mix of alcohol and witch hazel (a plant) extract that's often used as an astringent, or to soothe irritated skin.

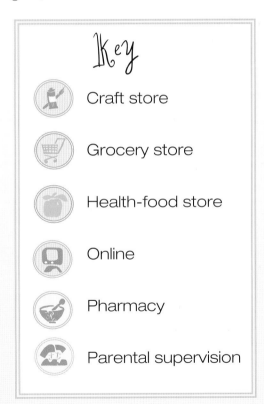

Key

Craft store

Grocery store

Health-food store

Online

Pharmacy

Parental supervision

*Note:*

*Many of the ingredients in this book are used over and over again in different recipes. Most ingredients are relatively inexpensive, but if you find that they cost too much for you, keep in mind that you can often substitute less expensive materials for the pricey ones.*

# A LITTLE BIT OF
## Science

As you get more comfortable with making the recipes, you'll find that it's easy to make substitutions. Ingredients fall into three categories: water based, oil based, and emulsifiers. A water-based ingredient is any liquid ingredient that dissolves and mixes with water. An oil-based ingredient is any ingredient that will dissolve and mix with oils. Oil and water won't stay mixed together without the use of an emulsifier. If you can't find a product that's listed on a recipe, see if you can find a substitute that falls into the same category. When substituting oils, try to find a replacement that is the same weight. For example, if you can't find shea butter, use cocoa butter instead. The texture will be slightly different, but if you keep the proportions the same, the recipe will still be successful.

### Water-Based Ingredients

Aloe vera gel

Aloe vera juice

Alcohol

Witch hazel

Rose water

Orange water

Glycerin

### Emulsifiers

Beeswax

Lecithin

Borax

Cornstarch

### Oil-Based Ingredients

Coconut oil

Almond oil

Light sesame oil

Grapeseed oil

Lanolin

Shea butter

Cocoa butter

## GLOSSARY

Here are a few words that you'll be hearing over and over again in the book. If you forget what they mean while you're reading, you can always turn back here to look them up again!

**ASTRINGENT.** An ingredient that removes oil and dirt from the skin.

**EXFOLIATE.** Removing dead, flaky layers of skin by scrubbing with a slightly gritty substance.

**EMOLLIENT.** Something that smoothes and softens the skin.

**EMULSIFY.** To mix two or more liquids together.

**EMULSIFIERS.** Ingredients used to bring oil-based and water-based ingredients together.

**MOISTURIZER.** A cream or lotion that makes skin less dry.

## RECIPE NOTES

● The recipes in this book can be easily cut in half or doubled if you want to make some for yourself and some for a friend.

● The amount of color and fragrance you want to add to your products is your choice. Experiment by adding fragrance and color a little at a time. You can always add more, but you can't take it away!

● When filling a container, leave a little extra room at the top. You want the container to be full, but not overflowing.

● There is one drawback to using all natural ingredients: they don't always have a long shelf life. Lotions and creams that use glycerin or oil and water together should be made in small batches since they will lose their freshness over time. Try adding a little citric acid (a natural preservative available through online natural cosmetics sites) to extend the life of your product.

# Fragrance
# FUNDAMENTALS

One of the best things about homemade natural beauty products is the wonderful way they smell. Smell is the strongest of our five senses, so it can have a powerful effect on us. Some people believe that fragrance can actually heal our minds and bodies (see the information on aromatherapy on pages 18 and 19). For many of the projects in the book, you'll be creating fragrances by mixing ingredients, including oils. Before you start making recipes, read about the different properties of the ingredients to help you decide what's best for you to use.

## Using Oils in Recipes

There are two types of oils used to make most fragrances in the recipes: essential oils and fragrance oils.

Essential oils are taken directly from plants and flowers, and there's nothing added to them. Since they're so pure, they're strong, and you need to use only a few drops to get a powerful fragrance. Some essential oils can irritate the skin though, so make sure you dilute them before using them (see page 17). Since essential oils are harvested from plants by hand, they can be expensive. But a little oil goes a long way, and the fragrance that they create is long lasting. Once you find an essential oil that you like, you may want to adapt the recipes in the book and use it in all of them. By having your own signature scent, you can also avoid having too many conflicting aromas.

Fragrance oils are the second option for adding fragrance to your projects. They're synthetic, meaning they're not natural. They're made by combining essential oils with chemicals or other oils. You can buy fragrance oils with a single fragrance (such as orange), or in a mixture of fragrances (such as orange-peppermint). How do you choose between essential oil and fragrance oil? If you're short on cash (and what girl isn't?), you might want to go for the cheapest thing you can find, which is usually a fragrance oil. But keep in mind that while some essential oils, such as orange, lemon, and peppermint cost about the same as fragrance oils, they last a lot longer. For more expensive scents like lavender, rose, or gardenia, you may want to go with the less expensive fragrance oil.

### ANOTHER OPTION

In addition to oils, you could try using soap fragrance in your recipes. This product is made specifically for use with homemade soaps, but it works well in other homemade beauty products, too. Soap fragrance is a synthetic (man-made) water-based fragrance rather than an oil-based fragrance, and it's less expensive than essential or fragrance oils.

There is one thing you shouldn't use, though. Don't use candle fragrances in your beauty products. They're not designed to be used on skin, so they could cause irritation.

## Safe Use of Essential Oils

● Essential oils contain strong natural chemicals and should be used with care. Never swallow an essential oil. Make sure to keep the oils away from your little brothers or sisters so they don't swallow them.

● Before using an essential oil on your skin, dilute it with almond oil or grapeseed oil.

● Always skin test an essential oil on a small patch of skin before using it. Each person's body is different, so you don't know how yours will react to it.

● Use essential oils sparingly. A little goes a very long way!

● Be careful about suntanning after using essential oils. Some make you more sun-sensitive.

● If you notice that you are having a strange reaction (like a rash on your skin or a headache), don't use the oil, and let your parents know immediately.

## WHAT IS AROMATHERAPY?

Have you ever walked into a room that smelled great, and you suddenly felt more relaxed or in a better mood? You may have been experiencing aromatherapy! When considering what fragrances to add to your projects, you may want to read up on aromatherapy. The idea behind aromatherapy is that herbs and plants not only smell great but can actually make you feel better physically and mentally. Most often aromatherapy fragrances are sprayed into the air, diffused through a candle to scent a room, or rubbed onto the skin like perfume.

The list of fragrances and their special aromatherapy qualities on page 19 will help you to decide which oils to use and which fragrances to blend. You'll find suggested scents for each project in the book, but as you get more familiar with the qualities of the different scents and begin to have a few favorites, you may want to branch out. You can easily use these recipes as a jumping-off point. Substituting fragrance is the easiest way to personalize the recipes in this book and make them your own!

## Aromatherapy

### Bergamot
Scent: fresh, sweet, and citrusy
Effect: relaxing, calming, and refreshing
Goes well with rose and gardenia

### Calendula
Scent: light herbal
Effect: cooling and soothing
Goes well with chamomile, lemongrass,
 and ginger

### Chamomile
Scent: fruity, herbal
Effect: relaxing and calming
Goes well with bergamot and lavender

### Eucalyptus
Scent: crisp and woody
Effect: stimulating
Goes well with lavender, rosemary, and orange

### Gardenia
Scent: strong floral
Effect: uplifting
Goes well with rose, bergamot, and jasmine

### Ginger
Scent: tart, sweet, and woody
Effect: warming and invigorating
Goes well with all citrus

### Honeysuckle
Scent: sweet, subtle floral
Effect: calming
Goes well with jasmine, rose, and peach

## Fragrances

### Jasmine
Scent: sweet, delicate floral
Effect: romantic and relaxing
Goes well with citrus and vanilla

### Lavender
Scent: fresh, light herbal, woody
Effect: relaxing, headache relief
Goes well with rosemary and lemongrass

### Mint
Scent: clean, cool, and fresh
Effect: refreshing and stimulating
Goes well with lemon, lavender, and rosemary

### Orange
Scent: fresh, citrusy
Effect: relaxing
Goes well with lavender, ginger, and peach

### Rose
Scent: soft, woody floral
Effect: comforting, uplifting, and relaxing
Goes well with lavender, jasmine, and bergamot

### Rosemary
Scent: woody, fresh
Effect: stimulating, calming
Goes well with lavender and lemon

### Vanilla
Scent: sweet, earthy
Effect: calming and uplifting, stimulates
appetite
Goes well with almost any fragrance

### Ylang-Ylang
Scent: super-sweet floral
Effect: deeply relaxing, very romantic
Goes well with jasmine

### WARNING!
Some essential oils are toxic. Please be careful when using them and check out any new essential oil before using it. The following is a list of essential oils that are very dangerous. Don't assume that an oil is safe just because it's not on this list! Most of these oils seem pretty stinky and unappealing anyway!

*Ajowan, Arnica, Bitter almond, Boldo leaf, Calamus, Camphor, Deertongue, Garlic, Horseradish, Jaborandi, Melilotus, Mugwort, Mustard, Onion, Pennyroyal, Rue, Sassafras, Spanish broom, Sweet birch, Thuja, Wintergreen, Wormseed, Wormwood*

# CONTAIN
## Yourself!

A great recipe with the best ingredients is only the start of a fantastic homemade beauty product. Once you've got that scent-sational perfume, what are you going to put it in? Part of the fun of making your own bath and beauty products is picking out a cool container. Look around your house for any empty or nearly empty bottles, tins, jars, or boxes. It's especially fun to use something unusual that was originally used for something else, like the paint can (buy a new one) used on page 69 or the little jelly jars on page 65. Best of all, these things are free! Just make sure you clean and dry the container first, and that you can find a lid. Most labels come off easily after soaking in hot water for a few minutes.

If you want a really special container, or you need to have a certain type of top (like a spray or pump top), check on the Internet for container compa-nies—there's a lot of cool stuff out there! If you order a container online, make sure that it's "cosmetic grade" or "food grade." That means it's safe to use for homemade products. Some containers that are meant for industrial use could be unsafe for your prod-ucts. Look for a company that has no minimum order, will sell containers individually or in small lots, and doesn't charge a lot.

## Labels and Other Embellishments

Now that you've got the right container, make a label to identify the product that's in it. Making labels can be really fun and creative. Look in the back of the book for some templates you can copy to make your own labels. Just photocopy the templates onto peel-and-stick label paper.

Once you've got your label, think of other embellishments for your container. You can add ribbons, paper, buttons, silk flowers, fabric, small plastic toys, or foam stickers, just to name a few.

Many craft stores carry miniature plastic gems, stationery miniatures, or sequined patches that you'll love using. It's *fun* to use your imagination and come up with a design that's completely unique.

# CREATE YOUR OWN *Spa Line*

Let's say you're crazy about a certain fragrance or ingredient, like lavender or rose. If you use your signature ingredient in a face cream, a body lotion, and a solid perfume, you've got your own personal "spa line" of products!

To make your spa products look special, make labels with the same designs and stick them onto the containers for each product. You can give all the products a similar name, such as "Rose Garden Soap" and "Rose Garden Hand Cream" etc., so they'll hold together as a group. Embellish the containers in a way that complements the name of the products: in the case of the rose garden line, you may want to put rose stickers or rose silk flowers on the containers. To get you started, we've created a set of label templates in the back of the book (page 124). Copy them onto peel-and-stick labels and personalize them with your own product names. A set of your homemade spa products makes a great gift that anyone will enjoy!

## Spa Party!

Making bath and beauty products is fun to do on your own, but it's even more fun with friends. Consider hosting a spa party so you and your friends can share the experience together. Invite each friend to bring her own favorite scent; you provide the rest of the ingredients for making great bath and beauty products. This is a fun activity for a sleepover, birthday party, or just a rainy day. You'll have a blast, and everyone will go home with some cool new products to use.

## Spa Kits

If you don't have time to round up all the ingredients you need, you can buy a kit at your local craft store that includes the supplies you need for a spa party with your friends. Often the kit contains a large supply of the basic ingredients, so you'll have some left over. This helps you to build a stash of materials so you can make lots of new projects.

# SAFETY IS Beautiful

You've got your recipes, ingredients, and containers, and you're ready to start making some fantastic beauty products. There's just one more thing you need to think about before you begin—how to be careful and avoid hurting yourself.

Most of these projects can be completed on your own without adult supervision, but when you see this symbol next to a project, it means you're going to need a grown-up around while you do the project.

With the exception of soap colors, all of the ingredients used in this book are natural and shouldn't cause a reaction; however, it's always good to be cautious. You may be sensitive to some of the ingredients and not even know it. Try the recipe on a small patch of your skin (somewhere like your forearm or stomach) first. You need to see if the recipe is going to cause a reaction before smearing it all over your face! If you are sensitive to fragrance or color, leave it out. It won't affect the outcome of the recipe.

Projects that require the use of a microwave, hot glue gun, or sewing machine can be dangerous, so PLEASE ask for help.

Always use your glue gun on a flat surface. It usually comes with a stand to keep it upright. Don't lay it down on the flat surface or it could catch fire. Keep your fingers away from the tip. Don't touch the glued spot until it cools down. Always keep a small glass of ice water within arm's reach when you're using a glue gun. Don't be tempted to reposition something that is coated in hot glue. Always unplug the hot glue gun or iron when you're finished using it.

Sewing machines can really hurt your fingers, so keep them out from under the needle area. If you get something stuck under the needle, unplug the machine before you try to get it out!

Don't exceed the recommended microwave heating times for the projects. The times are carefully calculated to melt the ingredients enough to mix them without boiling, but the ingredients are still very hot. Overheating could result in burning!

Keep the lid on a running blender or food processor. Remove the center plug when adding ingredients, but cover the hole as much as possible to keep the ingredients from splattering. Never stick your hand, fingers, or anything else into a running blender or food processor. Unplug the machine before you scrape down the sides.

Now that we've got that out of the way, let's start making some cool stuff!

# CHAPTER ONE

# Skin Care

Your skin is the only thing you're going to be wearing *all* day, *every* day for the rest of your life! Since you can't throw it in the laundry, take it to the dry cleaners, or trade it in, you'd better take good care of it so it will look great for a lifetime. Treat your skin like the wonderfully precious possession it is. Pamper it, protect it, and give it what it needs—plenty of TLC. Your local drugstore probably has shelf after shelf of creams, lotions, and potions all claiming to be just the thing your skin needs. But what do you *really* need? The answer is, none of it. If you take good care of your skin and make your own skin care products, you won't have to buy a lot of stuff (some of which doesn't really work anyway). Follow the skin care tips in this chapter, and try the recipes for easy-to-make skin care products. You'll have fun doing it, save money, and your skin will shine with a nice healthy glow.

# Orange Dream Face Cream

Before you go to bed at night, give your skin a big drink of this delicious orange-vanilla face cream. It's like a smoothie for your skin!

### 1
Combine the witch hazel, aloe vera gel, vanilla soap fragrance, and borax in blender or small bowl, and blend until the gel has liquefied and the borax has dissolved.

### 2
Combine the grapeseed oil and beeswax in a small glass measuring cup. Microwave for 30 seconds on high, then check every 20 seconds until the beeswax has completely melted.

### 3
With the blender still running, slowly drizzle the oil mixture into the aloe mix. Add the essential oil and soap color. Go slowly— if you pour it too fast the mix will separate. Mix really well, until the oil and water has emulsified and looks like mayonnaise.

### 4
Pour the mixture into the jars while it's still warm. It will set quickly as it cools.

## You Will Need

Small glass measuring cup

½ cup witch hazel

½ cup aloe vera gel

⅛ teaspoon borax

Measuring spoons

3 drops orange essential oil

3 drops vanilla soap fragrance

½ cup grapeseed oil

¼ cup grated beeswax or beeswax block and grater

Microwave

Blender or hand mixer and small bowl

2 to 3 drops of orange soap color

2 plastic containers, each 4 ounces

*Note: A food processor works best for making this cream. If you use a blender, just stop the motor often and scrape down the sides.*

*Note: This recipe makes slightly more than two 4-ounce jars. You can save the rest to make the Apricot Scrub (see page 45).*

# Bye, Bye, Dry Lotion Stick

This lotion targets super-dry places like knees and elbows with a concentrated zap of moisturizing power. Just rub it on and let it soak in. The container is great for travel, too, so keep it in your locker or gym bag for dry skin emergencies!

**1**
Place all ingredients together in a glass measuring cup.

**2**
Melt for 30 seconds on high in the microwave, then check every 20 seconds until melted.

**3**
Funnel the lotion into the dispenser, and let it cool.

## You Will Need

Glass measuring cup

Measuring spoons

Microwave

3 tablespoons grated beeswax or beeswax block and grater

2 tablespoons cocoa butter

2 tablespoons shea butter

4 tablespoons sweet almond oil

Solid lotion dispenser

Funnel

# What's Your Type?

When you look at skin care products in the store, you'll see that many of them are made for different skin "types:" normal, dry, and oily. But how do you know which skin type you have? Take a look at the descriptions below:

Normal skin produces just enough oil to keep it smooth and healthy, but not so much that it causes lots of breakouts.

Dry skin doesn't produce enough oil, leaving it tight feeling and sometimes flaky looking. It usually needs some exfoliating and extra moisturizing.

Oily skin produces way too much oil, leaving it shiny looking and prone to breakouts and enlarged pores. It needs extra deep cleaning to prevent breakouts.

You may also have combination skin. That means your skin is usually normal except for the T-zone—the area around your forehead, nose, and chin—where it tends to be oily.

To find out what kind of skin you have, take the following quiz. Answer Yes, No, or Sometimes to each question.

1. Do you get chapped skin in the winter?

2. Does your skin ever look flaky?

3. Do your elbows, knees, and feet feel rough?

4. Does your skin flake or peel?

5. Does your face look shiny when you wake up in the morning?

6. Do you tan easily?

7. Does your face sweat a lot?

8. Do you tend to break out?

9. Does your forehead, chin, or nose get shiny at the end of the day?

If you answered *Sometimes* to most questions, you probably have normal skin.

If you answered *Yes* to questions 1 to 4, you probably have dry skin.

If you answered *Yes* to questions 5 to you most likely have oily skin.

If you think that you have oily skin, ask yourself one more question. Is your face oily all over, or just in your T-zone? If it's just oily in your T-zone and normal everywhere else, you have combination skin.

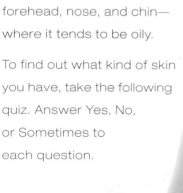

## Daily Routine for Normal Skin

Wash your face every day with a mild nondrying facial soap. If your skin is sensitive, try using a cream-based non-foaming facial cleanser.

Use a cotton ball to apply toner. It calms skin and removes any last traces of dirt after washing.

Moisturize your face with a lotion or cream suited to your skin type. Avoid getting moisturizer in your eyes.

## Daily Routine for Dry Skin

Drink lots of water. You need a lot of water every day, and your skin can't stay hydrated, no matter how much lotion you use, unless you drink about eight 8-ounce glasses of water a day. Sorry, sodas don't count. They actually dehydrate you more.

Shower quickly, and avoid using really hot water. It strips moisture and oils out of skin much faster than warm water. If you prefer taking a bath, skip the bubbles.

Exfoliate your skin once or twice a week. Use a gentle scubber like a natural sponge or a sugar scrub. Scrubs help to get rid of the dry, flaky patches of skin that cause itchiness.

Dry off lightly so your skin isn't soaking but it's still moist. Apply lots and lots of lotion.

## Daily Routine for Oily Skin

Cleanse your skin twice daily with a foaming cleanser, but avoid over-washing, which will over-strip your skin and cause it to produce more oil.

Exfoliate once a week to remove dead skin cells.

Use a clay mask to draw impurities from your skin. Again, don't do this every day. Once a week should be fine.

Use a very light moisturizer.

### T-ZONE TREATMENT

Use a clay mask on your T-zone only.

Avoid using a heavy moisturizer on your T-zone.

# Lemon Meringue Body Lotion

If you love the smell of lemons and the feeling of very soft skin, this is the body lotion for you. Make it as a gift for any lemon lovers you know.

### You Will Need

Measuring spoons

Glass measuring cup

$1/2$ cup aloe vera gel

$1/4$ cup water

2 tablespoons glycerin

$1/2$ to 1 teaspoon borax

Small bowl

Blender or hand mixer

$3/4$ cup grapeseed oil

$1/2$ cup grated beeswax or beeswax block and grater

1 teaspoon lanolin

Microwave

10 drops lemon essential oil, fragrance oil, or soap fragrance

3 to 6 drops yellow soap color

8-ounce plastic container

**1**

Combine the aloe vera gel, water, glycerin, and borax in a small bowl, and blend with a hand mixer until the gel has liquefied and the borax has dissolved.

**2**

Combine the grapeseed oil, beeswax, and lanolin in a small glass measuring cup. Microwave for 30 seconds on high, then check every 20 seconds until the beeswax and lanolin are completely melted.

**3**

With the hand mixer on high, slowly drizzle the grapeseed oil mix into the aloe mix. Add the essential oil. Go slowly—if you pour too fast, the mixes will separate instead of coming together. Mix really well until the oil and water have emulsified (see page 15) and the mix looks like mayonnaise.

**4**

Add the soap color.

**5**

Pour the mix into the container while it's still warm. It will set quickly as it cools.

*Note: A hand mixer works best for making this project. If you use a blender, just stop the motor often and scrape down the sides.*

# Mud Pie Clay Mask

## You Will Need

Measuring cup

½ cup French green clay

½ cup bentonite (white) clay

½ cup Moroccan red clay

1½ cups cornstarch

Sifter

3 glass jars (each should hold about 1 cup of clay)

Glass mixing bowl

Spoon

Clay isn't just for art class. There are special cosmetic clays that are used for facial masks to give your skin a deep cleaning. This recipe combines three kinds of clays to suck the dirt and grime right out. French green clay draws impurities from your skin. It's great for blackheads or frequent breakouts. Moroccan red clay is used for exfoliating dead skin cells that make your skin look dull and flaky. Bentonite (white) clay is great for tightening your skin and shrinking up enlarged pores.

## 1
Sift the green clay and ½ cup of cornstarch together into a small bowl. Transfer it into one of the glass jars.

## 2
Sift the red clay and ½ cup of cornstarch together into a small bowl. Transfer it into one of the glass jars.

## 3
Sift the white clay and ½ cup of cornstarch together into a small bowl. Transfer it into one of the glass jars.

### TO USE

## 1
Spoon about 2 tablespoons of the clay mixture you want to use into a small cup.

## 2
Add just enough water to make a thick paste. It should be spreadable, but not runny.

## 3
Spread the mixture evenly over your face.

## 4
Kick back with a book for a few minutes while the mask works its magic. Don't let the mask dry on your face. It could overdry your skin.

## 5
Rinse off the mask with warm water.

# Zit's

## Not as Bad as It Seems

Zits happen, and unless you're very lucky, sooner or later they'll happen to you. But just because you get the occasional break-out doesn't mean you're doomed to spend your preteen and teen years hiding your face and avoiding contact with all other human life forms. There are plenty of ways you can minimize the number of zits you get and treat the ones you do get so they quickly disappear.

## Where Do They Come From?

Zits are caused by plugged-up pores. We all have very small hairs covering our skin (we *are* mammals, you know). When a small hair plugs up a skin pore or follicle, a mixture of oil, bacteria, and dead skin cells builds up behind the plug, causing it to become very sore and red.

Eventually, the plugged-up pore builds up above the surface of the skin, and you'll see a pimple, *aka* zit.

Why do pores get plugged?

Here are some reasons:

Changing hormone levels

Greasy, heavy cosmetics

Air pollution

Squeezing or picking zits

Scrubbing too hard when you wash your skin

## Stop Them Before They Start

Keeping your skin clean is the first step to preventing zits. Wash your face with a mild soap before bed. You may have heard the expression "squeaky clean." In the case of skin, squeaky clean is something you want to avoid. If your skin squeaks when you rub it after washing, it's too dry. Dry skin signals to your body that it needs to make more oil, which can lead to more clogged pores and more breakouts.

Every time you touch your face, the oil and dirt from your hands transfers onto your face—yuck.

This can lead to clogged pores and breakouts. Try to keep your hands clean, too, or at least keep them away from your face.

## They're Here!

Well, you tried your best, but your face broke out anyway. Now what?

A cool washcloth or a pad soaked in witch hazel will remove redness and dry out your zit a little. Try to keep some cotton balls soaked in witch hazel in a plastic bag in your fridge so you'll have them when you need them.

Don't attack your face! Never squeeze a pimple, it will only make it worse, and it might also scar your skin. A warm washcloth will help bring a pimple to a head—that means whatever is inside will come out.

Try using a light exfoliating scrub (see pages 40, 41, and 45 for more info) on areas prone to breakouts, but don't scrub too hard. You may end up damaging your skin and causing more breakouts instead of making it better.

If, after taking all these steps, your pimple problem doesn't seem to get better, talk to your parents about seeing a dermatologist. He or she will be able to identify what's going on and help you with medication or a new skin care routine.

## Zit Myths and Facts

We've all heard the stories: if you eat chocolate, your face will break out. Eating pizza will cause your face to look like a pizza. But how much of this is really true? Check the list below for the real scoop.

**MYTH**
Eating chocolate, junk food, and greasy food causes pimples.

**FACT**
Unless you have food allergies, food won't cause a breakout.

**MYTH**
Dirty skin causes acne.

**FACT**
Pimples are not caused by dirt, but clogged pores.

**MYTH**
Getting stressed-out can cause a breakout.

**FACT**
Stress does not cause pimples; it's just a coincidence.

**MYTH**
Only kids get zits.

**FACT**
Although zits are more common in teenagers, plenty of adults get them too.

**MYTH**
You can only get pimples on your face.

**FACT**
Zits don't just happen on your face; you can also get them on your arms, neck, back, chest, and shoulders.

# Orange Spa Line

# Orange Delight Body Lotion

Smooth a dollop of this rich
creamy lotion onto your skin after
your bath or shower.
You'll feel softer in seconds
and you'll smell fantastic too.

**1**
Combine the water and borax in
a blender and pulse until the borax
is dissolved.

**2**
Combine the grapeseed oil and
beeswax in a small glass measuring cup.
Microwave for 30 seconds on high,
then check every 20 seconds until the
beeswax is completely melted.

**3**
With the blender or hand mixer running,
slowly drizzle the oil mixture into the
water mix. Mix really well, until the oil and
water have emulsified.

**4**
Add the essential oil and color, and stir
or mix to combine.

**5**
Pour the lotion into the container.

## You Will Need

Small glass measuring cup

¾ cup water

½ teaspoon borax

Blender or hand mixer

¾ cup grapeseed oil

Measuring spoon

3 tablespoons grated beeswax or
beeswax block and grater

Microwave

10 drops sweet orange essential oil,
fragrance oil, or soap fragrance

5 to 6 drops orange soap color

Funnel

16-ounce container

# Orange Fizz Face Wash for Dry Skin

Dry skin needs to be clean, but washing it with ordinary soap only makes it feel tighter and drier. This wash is a perfect solution: it leaves your skin clean and moist, and as an extra bonus, it smells great!

## You Will Need

Measuring cup

Measuring spoons

¼ cup witch hazel

¼ cup aloe vera gel

¼ cup glycerin

⅛ teaspoon borax

Blender

10 drops orange essential oil or fragrance oill

10 drops vanilla essential oil or fragrance oil

5 drops orange liquid soap color

2 tablespoons grated clear glycerin soap, melted

Small bowl

Microwave

Funnel

10-ounce container

1

Place the witch hazel, aloe vera gel, glycerin, and borax in a blender, and pulse until the ingredients are combined.

2

Add the essential oil (or fragrance oil) and color. Mix really well—until the oil and water emulsify (see page 15).

3

Melt the glycerin soap in a microwave.

4

Remove the mix from the blender and slowly stir in the melted soap.

5

Pour the mixture into the bottle using the funnel.

# Citrus Splash Toner

You know that fresh, crisp taste you get when you bite into a really good, juicy slice of orange? This toner feels just like that on your skin. Whether your skin is normal, oily, or dry, a toner helps to calm and balance it after cleansing and before you moisturize.

## You Will Need

6 ounces orange water

2 ounces witch hazel

2 drops orange essential oil

2 drops vanilla essential oil, fragrance oil, or soap fragrance

8-ounce dispenser bottle

**1**
Combine all ingredients in the mister bottle, and shake well.

**2**
Mist the toner over your face or apply it with a cotton ball after cleansing.

# Sugar Bear Face and Body Scrub

At the end of the day does your face feel as dirty as the bottom of your shoes? Scrub off that grime with this gentle, sweet-smelling scrub. Salt scrubs can be too harsh to use on your face, but this sugar scrub is mild enough for even super-sensitive skin.

## You Will Need

Measuring cup

1 cup brown sugar

1 cup white sugar

Small bowl

Mixing spoon

Sweet almond oil

Sweet orange essential oil, fragrance oil, or soap fragrance

Container of your choice

**1**

Place the sugar in a small bowl.

**2**

Slowly add the sweet almond oil to the sugar until it starts to look like a thick paste.

**3**

Add the essential oil a few drops at a time until it smells just right. Put the scrub in a decorative container.

Use this scrub once or twice a week on wet skin. Gently rub dry or dull patches with a small palm full of scrub. Avoid rubbing too hard, as it can cause redness or irritation.

## The Tough Slough Test

If your skin is really dry, you need to exfoliate or slough (pronounced *sluff*) it—that means remove the dead skin. But since sloughing can be rough on skin, take this test first to make sure you need to do it.

Take a piece of scotch tape and press it onto your forehead. Gently peel it off and look at the tape. If it looks really dull and has a lot of flaky stuff on it, your skin is ready for a good sloughing. Use a gentle scrub like the recipe above, or wash your face with a natural sponge and a mild soap. Be gentle or your skin may get raw and irritated. After you exfoliate, your skin will look much healthier.

# Honey Almond Body Butter

This body cream looks and smells good enough to eat! Don't try it though—it's meant to feed your thirsty skin, not your tummy.

### 1
Combine the glycerin, fragrance, and borax in a blender, and pulse until the borax is dissolved.

### 2
Combine the sweet almond oil, shea butter, cocoa butter, and beeswax in a small glass measuring cup. Microwave for 30 seconds on high, then check every 20 seconds until the beeswax is completely melted.

### 3
With the blender running, slowly drizzle the oil mixture into the glycerin mix. Go slowly—if you pour it too fast, the mix will separate. Mix really well until the oil and glycerin have emulsified (see page 15) and the mixture is thick and creamy.

### 4
Pour the mixture into the jar while it's warm. It will set quickly and harden as it cools.

## You Will Need

Glass measuring cup

Measuring spoons

½ cup glycerin

10 drops honey almond soap fragrance

½ teaspoon borax

Blender

½ cup sweet almond oil

2 tablespoons shea butter

¼ cup cocoa butter

3 tablespoons grated beeswax or beeswax block and grater

Microwave

8-ounce jar

## Be a Fridge Face!

Fruits and vegetables aren't just for eating. They're also great for making cleansing masks for your face. Different fruits and vegetables have different qualities, so look at the list below to find out what kind of mask you need. What a cool beauty supply store you have in your fridge!

Grapes firm your skin and are slightly astringent. Just mash them and blend them with enough apple juice to make a thick paste to spread over your face.

Applesauce is cooling and astringent. You can just apply it directly to your face.

Strawberries and kiwis have lots of vitamin C and are good for removing excess oil from oily skin. Mash them into a paste and leave it on your face for a few minutes.

Mashed avocado and bananas are fantastic for moisturizing dry skin. Spread the mask over your face, and leave it for a few minutes. Rinse it off and pat dry.

It may sound unappealing, but mayonnaise makes a great quick facial mask. It's got all of the oils and protein that really dry skin needs. Smear it on and wait for about 20 minutes, then rinse.

Mashed tomatoes are good for refining pores and drawing out impurities. Try spreading some on your face.

For a quick exfoliating scrub, mix 1 tablespoon honey, 1 tablespoon cornmeal, and 1 tablespoon of milk. Let it thicken for a few minutes, and then gently massage it over your face and neck. Rinse with warm water and pat dry.

If your skin is super oily, make a mask by beating one egg white with an electric mixer until the egg white is stiff and holds its shape. Spread it over your face and leave it for 20 minutes. Rinse and wash your face as usual. Your skin will be oil-free for days.

Plain yogurt is great for soothing red, aggravated skin. Just spread it on.

Up a little too late last night studying for the big exam? Place a slice of potato or cucumber over each eye, and rest for about 15 minutes. Now those dark circles are history!

# Sun SOS
## (Save Our Skin!)

Sitting in the sun is a great feeling. But unless you're protecting your skin while you're out in the sun, you can get too much of a good thing. The sun's rays (ultraviolet A [UVA] and ultraviolet B [UVB]) can cause serious damage to your skin. Exposure to UVA and UVB rays can lead to wrinkles or even skin cancer.

A sunburn happens when your skin is damaged by overexposure to UVB rays. If you've been in the sun too long, the blood vessels close to the surface of the skin get damaged and swollen, which is why the skin looks red and is painful to touch. The reddening starts soon after exposure, and usually lasts for three to four days. The burn damages the top layer of skin, which is what causes it to dry up and peel off. While the peeling lasts for only a few days, the damage is permanent. Exposure to UVB rays is the main cause of skin cancer.

UVA rays go deeper into the skin to produce a tan, but too much exposure to UVA rays can cause sunburn as well. A tan is the skin's attempt to protect itself from the sun's harmful rays, so even if you don't burn, too much sun can lead to skin cancer.

If you want to look tan without damaging your skin, try using a self-tanning product (available at department stores). The trick to making your bottled tan look natural is to exfoliate and use lots of moisturizer before applying the self-tanner. Rub the self-tanning lotion onto your skin in a thin, smooth, even layer. It's always best to apply several light coats over a few days so you don't end up with streaks and blotches on your skin. Always wash your hands afterwards or it will turn your palms and nails dark brown. Using tan-in-a-tube will help you get the look you want without damaging your skin.

# Apricot Face Scrub

If you make the Orange Dream Face Cream on page 26, you'll have some great stuff left over after you fill your containers. Don't throw it out! You can use it to make this scrub that gently exfoliates and leaves your skin feeling soft.

## You Will Need

Measuring cup

Measuring spoons

Small bowl

¼ cup leftover face cream

2 tablespoons melted opaque glycerin soap

2 tablespoons ground apricot kernels

Small jar

### 1
Combine all ingredients in a small bowl and stir.

### 2
Store your scrub in a small jar.

# Beauty
### Inside and Out

You may think you know the perfect girl: perfect hair, perfect skin, and perfect clothes. But all those things don't really tell you much about beauty. It's what's inside—qualities like kindness, loyalty, humor, and generosity—that really makes a person beautiful. They shine out from the inside and make you want to be with a person. Hairstyles and fashions change all the time, but being a good friend will always make you look great!

## Mirror, Mirror on the Wall,
# Is That Really Me?

What do you see when you look in the mirror? Sometimes we tend to focus on the things we don't like instead of the things we do. We exaggerate the parts we think are "flaws," making them seem so big that we can't imagine everyone else doesn't notice how bad they are. Meanwhile, we overlook the parts we like the best, thinking that our least favorite part must be the one everyone notices. Next time you look in the mirror, choose the thing you like best about your looks (and yes, everyone has at least one—what about your eyes, your hair, your smile…?) and focus on that instead. You may find out there's a lot more to like than you ever realized.

# Seaside Salt Scrub

Salt is a great natural exfoliator, especially for those really tough scaly patches. This scrub will really take off that flaky skin, but don't use it on your legs if you plan to shave.

## You Will Need

Measuring cup

1 cup fine-ground sea salt

1/2 cup sweet almond oil

5 drops ginger essential oil

5 drops grapefruit essential oil

8-ounce glass jar

Place all of the ingredients in the plastic container, and stir well.

CHAPTER TWO

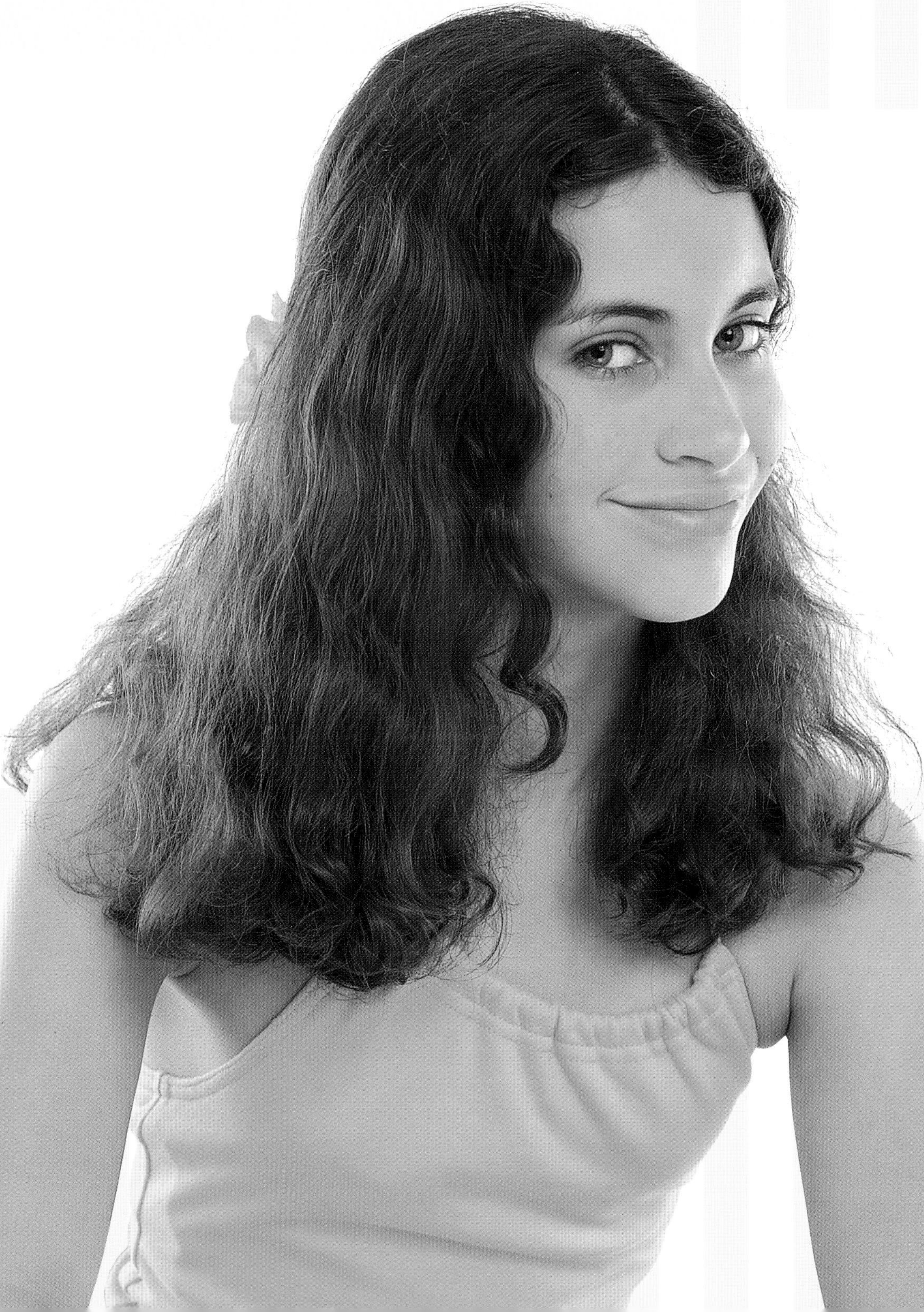

# Hair Care

K, let's review: the skin you're in now is going to

be with you forever, so you need to take good

care of it. But what about your hair? It changes

all the time! From the time you were born until now, your

hair has probably been different shades or even entirely

different colors. It may have been curly when you were

a baby, but could be straight as a stick now.

Your hair may seem to have a mind of its own.

One day it will sit happily inside a clip,

the next day it refuses to be tamed, and falls down in

your face. Hair can be unpredictable, but that's also

what makes it fun to experiment with. Try the recipes

in this chapter for some wonderful shampoos,

conditioners, and other treatments, or make the

cool hair gear. We also give you some great secret

hair-care tips!

# Shampoo Line

Try making your own shampoo with the *great* recipes on page 51 and 52.

# Eucalyptus-Mint Shampoo

Eucalyptus and mint smell fresh and have
natural cleansing properties for hair. This
shampoo is perfect for normal to oily hair.
Since it's made with all-natural ingredients,
you'll need to use it within two weeks of
making it before the natural
elements start to go bad. You can get
about 10 shampoos out of this recipe.

## You Will Need

Glass measuring cup

Measuring spoons

1 1/2 cups water

Bowl

Microwave

3 teaspoons grated glycerin soap

2 teaspoons glycerin

10 drops green soap color

1 drop blue soap color

10 drops peppermint
essential or fragrance oil

10 drops tea tree oil

3 drops eucalyptus
essential or fragrance oil*

Small plastic bottle

**1**
Bring 1 1/2 cups of water to a
boil in a bowl in the microwave.

**2**
Add the grated soap, and let
stand until the soap softens.

**3**
Stir in the glycerin until the
mixture is well blended.

**4**
Add the color and fragrance
until you get the look you want.

**5**
Pour the mixture into a bottle.

# Peachy Clean Shampoo

The sweet crisp scent of a ripe, juicy peach can be yours all day when you wash your hair with peachy clean shampoo. It leaves your hair fresh, adds a little bounce, and reminds you of a summer day.

**1**
Bring 1½ cups of water to a boil in a small saucepan.

**2**
Remove from heat and add the grated glycerin soap.

**3**
Let stand until the soap softens.

**4**
Stir in glycerin until mixture is well blended.

**5**
Add color, fragrance, and glitter if you like.

**6**
Pour into a bottle.

## You Will Need

Measuring cup

Small saucepan

1½ cups water

⅓ cup grated glycerin soap

2 tablespoons glycerin

Yellow liquid soap color

Peach liquid soap color

Lemongrass liquid soap fragrance

Orange liquid soap fragrance

Peach liquid soap fragrance

Cosmetic grade glitter (optional)

Small plastic bottle

# Naturally Beautiful Hair through
## Herbs

You may know that herbs are good for your skin and hair,
but how do you know which herbs do what?
Check this list of herbs and their hair-care specialties.

**Chamomile** leaves hair soft and shiny.

**Catnip** and **nasturtium** encourage
hair growth.

**Lavender** and **rosemary**
leave hair smelling fabulous.

**Rosemary** fluffs up limp hair.

**Sage** conditions and strengthens
damaged hair.

**Burdock root** helps to
heal a dry,
flaky scalp.

**Marigold** and
**mullein** lighten
blond hair.

**Witch hazel** degreas-
es normal to oily hair.

Think about making
a hair tea for your tresses.
Bring 3 cups of water to a boil.
Turn off the heat, and add ½ cup of herbs to the water,
then allow to steep until cool. Strain the mix into a plastic pitcher. Add ⅓-cup
vinegar. Pour the mixture over your hair as a final rinse after you condition.

# Hair Massage Deep Conditioning Treatment

Have you been experimenting with your hair a little *too* much? If you use a lot of styling products or blow dry, hot roll, or iron your hair a lot, it can dry out, frizz, or break. Try this hot oil treatment to help it heal. While it's drying, blow a little low heat onto your hair. It will look super glossy and shiny.

## 1
Mix all ingredients in a bowl and heat in microwave.

## 2
Cool slightly, and pour into the bottle.

### TO USE

Comb the conditioner through wet or dry hair. Put your hair in a plastic shower cap, or wrap your hair with plastic wrap. Wrap your hair in a towel, and leave it on for 15 to 20 minutes. Shampoo and condition as usual.

## You Will Need

Measuring cup

⅛ cup sweet almond oil

⅛ cup coconut oil

1 teaspoon glycerin

4 capsules of vitamin E oil

½ teaspoon lanolin

Bowl

Microwave

Small glass bottle

Shower cap or plastic wrap

# A Curl's Best Friend

Curly hair needs special care. Try these tips to keep your super-curly hair looking its best.

- Comb your hair while it's still wet, then rub some strong hold gel evenly through your hair. Starting close to the roots, scrunch your hair and separate your curls into ringlets to give it some bounce. Don't comb or brush your hair after it's dried, or it will POOF!

- If you need to dry your hair fast, use a blow drier with a diffuser, then twirl strands into ringlets.

- If your hair is curly and fine, a layered cut will give your curls more definition and bounce.

- Loosely braid your hair before you go to sleep so you don't wake up with a big mat of hair on the back of your head.

- To refresh your hair in the morning, run your hands under the faucet or use a spritzer to wet your hair, then scrunch it or twist it into ringlets. If you want, rub some gel into it, but don't comb it!

- If your hair gets more and more frizzy as the day progresses, try rubbing a teaspoon of aloe vera gel and some water between the palms of your hands and scrunching your hair. It will put the bounce back in your curls without making your hair sticky.

- If you hair is really tangled between shampoos, spritz it until it's really wet and load it up with a super-duper leave-in detangler. Then you can slowly pick untangle your hair, starting at the ends and working up towards the roots.

# The Cutting Edge

Choosing a haircut can seem like a major decision. A haircut can really change the way you look and affect the way you feel about your appearance. But if you get a less-than-perfect cut, don't worry. The great thing about hair is, it grows back! No change is ever permanent, so you'll only have to wait a matter of weeks for it to grow longer. To get the most out of your haircut, read the following advice.

Plan your next haircut. Cut pictures out of magazines, and bring them to your stylist. Talk with your stylist about your likes and dislikes. Make sure you're comfortable before the cutting begins. It's better to ask a lot of questions first than to be unhappy later.

If you're super active, consider choosing a hairdo that looks good, but doesn't need a lot of care.

A good cut can do wonders. If you can't grow your hair long without it looking straggly, go for a shorter look.

If you are uncertain about making a big change, make a gradual one. Go shorter over a period of several haircuts so that the difference doesn't seem like a big shock.

Whether your hair is short or long, it's important to keep the ends trimmed. If you start having a lot of really bad hair days, it's probably time for a trim.

## Hair Has Types, Too

In Chapter One, we talked about different types of skin. But hair has types, too, and like the skin types, the hair types are: dry, oily, and normal. Do you know which type yours is? Try this little experiment:

The day after you wash your hair, check out the patch of hair right over your ears. Rub it with a little piece of lotion-free tissue. If the tissue looks dry, you have dry hair. If the tissue is a little smudgy looking, but all of the strands still separate when you comb your hair, your hair is normal. If the tissue is oily looking, and the strands of your hair clump together when you comb it, you have oily hair.

Now that you know what type you have, how do you deal with it? Normal hair can do fine with a regular hair-care routine (see top of next page), but dry or oily hair needs special treatment (see the bottom of the page).

## Basic Hair-Care Routine
### for Normal Hair

As you reach puberty, chances are your scalp is going to start producing more oil. You may need to begin washing your hair more frequently. How often you need to shampoo depends on how much oil your scalp produces. You might need to shampoo once a day, every other day, or once a week. Be careful not to over-wash your hair. If you over-wash, your scalp will produce more oil, making your hair even greasier!

When washing, make sure your hair is fully soaked with water. Add mild shampoo, and massage it into a thick lather. Leftover soap residue attracts dirt, so rinse fully to avoid dull sticky hair. Apply a light conditioner, and then rinse again.

Choose a shampoo for your specific hair type. If your hair has been zapped by too much sun and chlorine, use a shampoo for dry and damaged hair. Don't be fooled into thinking that baby shampoo is mild. It's designed to remove dry flaky skin from a baby's scalp and is quite harsh.

## Oily
### Hair Care

If you have oily skin, you'll probably have oily hair as well. Oily hair is caused by overactive oil glands on your scalp. If you have oily hair, it probably needs to be washed frequently, maybe even every day. You might need to use a shampoo made just for oily hair, but be careful not to over-strip it. Over-stripping hair of natural oil can cause it to produce even more oil to make up for what it's lost.

## Dry
### Hair Care

Too much sun, harsh shampoos, chemical processing, or underactive oil glands on your scalp can cause dry hair. If you have really dry hair, condition it with warm herbal oil or a deep conditioning treatment (see page 54) at least twice a week. Avoid using harsh shampoos, since they can strip your hair and scalp of its protective oils. Try not to use electric curlers, straightening irons, and hair dryers.

# Hair Gear

If you're bored with your hair, it's growing out, or it's being

temperamental, try taming it with a

few easy-to-make accessories.

They also make great gifts!

## You Will Need

Hair ties

Waxed cotton string

Buttons

Scissors

Fabric tape measure

Pencil

Different colors of suede

Leather flower shape with central hole

Leather hole punch and small hammer

Thin leather cords, each 36 inches long

## FOR BUTTON HAIR TIES

Attach a button to the hair tie with the waxed cotton string. Pull the string snuggly before tying in the back. Trim the ends.

## FOR THE FLOWER HAIR TIE

Tie a leather cord to the ha tie, forming a knot at the er Push the knot through the center of the leather flowe shape to hold it in place.

## FOR THE SUEDE KERCHIEF

**1**

To determine the size of the kerchief, measure the distance between your ears—start at one ear and measure across the top of your head to the other ear. Write down this measurement.

**2**

Draw a light pencil line suede the same length as this measurement on the suede.

**3**

Fold the suede in half with ends touching, and draw a small mark to mark the center point. Using the width measurement, measure down from the center point to the tip. Connect this point with the points on either side.

**4**

Cut the suede into a large triangle.

**5**

Use the leather punch and the hammer (to drive it in) to make a hole about ½ inch in from each end of the long edge of the triangle. Continue making holes about 1 inch apart across the long edge.

**6**

Thread the leather strips through the holes.

# Hair-Brain-Ideas

## Hair-Care Secrets

Try a dry shampoo when you don't have time for the real thing (or you're on a camping trip and can't spare the water). Mix 3 tablespoons cornstarch with 2 drops of rosemary essential oil. Sprinkle your hair with the cornstarch mixture, and wait for 15 minutes. Now brush your hair really well and style it as usual. This trick works best on lighter hair. Try testing the idea first to see how your hair reacts (in other words, better not to try it for the first time on picture day!).

Shampoos, conditioners, and styling products can leave a build-up on hair that can make it hang down limp.

When this happens, try rinsing your hair after you shampoo with a mix of ⅓ cup vinegar and 1 cup water. It will leave your hair shiny and full of body.

If you have problems with an itchy, flaky scalp, try massaging your scalp with apple cider vinegar before you shampoo. Let it dry for a few minutes, then wash as usual.

Here is a quick fix for dandruff: Mix ¼ cup lime juice with ¼ cup coconut oil and massage it into your scalp. Wrap your head in plastic wrap, and give it some time to work. Shampoo after 1 hour.

## Hair Dos and Don'ts

● Don't overprocess your hair with chemicals. Perms, straightening, and color treatments can damage hair.

● Don't brush your hair when it's wet. The hair strands will snap, leaving you with fly-a-ways. Try using a wide-toothed comb instead.

● Do clean your hairbrush every once in a while. A dirty brush leads to limp, oily hair. Remove any stray hairs, and soak your brushes and combs overnight in warm water with a little baking soda added. In the morning, add a dash of shampoo to the water, and swish to make suds. Rinse and drip dry your brushes and combs.

## Bad Hair Day= Hip Hat Day

We all have them once in a while—the days when your hair unexpectedly starts doing exactly what you don't want it to do. Maybe it's the weather (humidity and rain can really make hair freak out), or maybe it's that new shampoo you just tried. Whatever the reason, you end up wanting to hide your hair until you can go home, wash it, and start all over again. How 'bout a hat? Hats are great fashion accessories that can really give you a distinctive look. A bad hair day is a great day to try one.

## Is Your Hair Overdone by the Sun?

When you go out on the beach you sensibly cover up with sunscreen to protect your skin. But what about your hair? After a day of fun in the sun, your hair can look frizzy and frazzled—the hair equivalent of a sunburn!

If your hair is really dry or chemically treated, you probably need some hair sunscreen next time you go to the beach. This mixture will block about 30 to 40 percent of the sun's damaging rays and keep it from drying out.

To make hair sunscreen, try the following recipe: Mix 3 tablespoons each of sesame oil and coconut oil with the contents of three vitamin E capsules. Comb the mixture through your hair and leave it on all day long. At the end of the day, shampoo and condition as usual. Your hair will be ultra-soft and super-conditioned.

# CHAPTER THREE

# Bath

Whether you're a bath person or a shower person, there are plenty of products out there to make you feel clean, smell great, and give you a fresh sensation. Store-bought is fine, but homemade is better. Bath products are fun to make and fun to give as presents. Try creating a soap or a bath bomb for a friend or a shower spray for your mom. And don't forget to treat yourself right too!

# Aromatherapy Bath Oils

If you've never explored aromatherapy (see page 18 for more info), here's you chance. People use aromatherapy scents to create a certain feeling or help fix a certain physical problem, like a headache or exhaustion. Sprinkle a few drops of these aromatherapy oils into your bathwater to see what magic they can work for you.

**1**
Place 25 drops each of the essential oils into each bottle.

**2**
Fill each bottle up to the neck with sweet almond oil. Be careful not to overfill.

**3**
Replace the dropper tops, and shake.

**4**
Personalize the bottles with labels that reflect the properties of the bath oil, or add beads and wire around the neck of the bottles to dress them up.

Lavender is uplifting if you're feeling down.

Rose is very calming if you're stressed out.

Ginger grapefruit is good for sore muscles.

Peppermint is reviving if you're exhausted!

## You Will Need

Sweet almond oil

Lavender essential oil

Grapefruit essential oil

Peppermint essential oil

Small blue dropper bottles

Small funnel

# Bath Jam

For a fun and fragrant addition to your bath, try a bath jam. Don't worry, it won't float on top, and you certainly don't have to add peanut butter! It dissolves into the water, leaving your skin soft, refreshed, and smelling great. Be careful as you make your bath jam—the ingredients can cause stains on towels and clothing.

### 1
Cut the soap into cubes, and melt it in a glass measuring cup in the microwave.

### 2
Mix aloe vera, witch hazel, and glycerin together. Stir gently to avoid making bubbles.

### 3
Pour the mixture into two separate jars. Add the powdered drink mix. The bath jam will set as it cools.

## You Will Need

Microwave

Knife

Glass measuring cup

1/2 cup clear glycerin soap

1/2 cup aloe vera gel

1/2 cup witch hazel

1/4 cup glycerin

2 packets of unsweetened powdered drink mix in the flavor of your choice

2 jelly jars

# Tea Time Bath Tea Bags

A bathtub and a cup of tea have more in common than you might think. After all, they're both filled with hot water, and they're both used for relaxation. Make a special bath tea bag for your tub, and let the herbs seep and fill it with a fragrant aroma. Then soak in it, enjoy it, but don't drink it!

## You Will Need

Mixture of dried herbs (see ideas below)

Scissors

White non-fusible fabric interfacing

Ruler or measuring tape

Iron and ironing board

Iron-on fabric hem tape

Hot glue gun and glue sticks

10-inch pieces of cotton string, one for each tea bag

Patterned paper

Stapler

## To Make the Bags

### 1

Cut four 15 x 10-inch pieces of the non-fusible fabric interfacing.

### 2

Place one piece of the interfacing on the ironing board. Fold the long edges into the center of the interfacing, overlapping them slightly in the center.

### 3

Tear off a 15-inch piece of iron-on hem tape. Place the tape between the two layers of the interfacing and press until it fuses.

### 4

Fold the interfacing in half with right sides together, and press. Fold each side back 1 inch, and press again. At this point if you hold the interfacing up and look at it from the side, it will resemble a W that is small at the bottom with two long "arms."

### 5

Trim the top edges so they're even.

### 6

Secure the bottom with two small dots of hot glue.

### 7

Fill the bag with a handful of mixed herbs in both side pockets.

### 8

Place the bag on a flat surface. Fold the top corners into the center, and then fold the top point down. Place one end of the cotton string down on top of this flap, and secure it with a staple.

### 9

Cut a 1 x 2-inch piece of paper. Fold it in half. Place the other end of the string into the open end, and secure it with a staple.

FOR THE HERBAL MIXTURE
IN A BOWL, MIX YOUR DRIED HERBS. TRY ONE OF THE FOLLOWING RECIPES:

• Mix equal parts spearmint and peppermint.

• Mix equal parts ginger, lemon peel, hibiscus, and lemongrass.

• Mix equal parts rosehips, orange peels, hibiscus, and cloves.

• Use lavender by itself.

# Apple Blossom After-Shower Mist

After your shower when you're feeling your freshest, spritz on this cool, refreshing spray that leaves a slight apple fragrance on your skin for hours. This spray is slightly astringent, so it's perfect for oily skin.

## You Will Need

Funnel
8-ounce plastic spray bottle
Measuring spoons
Measuring cup
2 tablespoons aloe vera gel
1/3 cup witch hazel
1 drop yellow soap color
3 drops lime green soap color
3 drops green apple fragrance oil
Distilled water

1
Funnel the aloe gel and the witch hazel into the spray bottle.

2
Add the soap color and the fragrance oil.

3
Fill up the bottle with distilled water and shake well.

# Lemon Squeeze Bath Salts

There's nothing like the feeling of a nice warm bath at the end of the day. Add a salt soak to your bath as an extra treat. It will leave your skin smooth as silk and soothe your sore muscles, too. Since epsom salts can be dehydrating, drink a glass of water as you soak.

## You Will Need

Measuring cup
Measuring spoons
Small bowls
2 cups sea salt
1 cup epsom salt
1 cup baking soda
2 tablespoons glycerin
Lemon essential oil
Small cellophane bag
1-quart size unused paint can
Paint-can opener
Ball chain
2 large sheets of yellow scrapbook paper, each in a different pattern
2 small wooden daisies
Scissors
Rubber cement
Hot glue gun and glue sticks

**1**
Mix all of the dry ingredients together.

**2**
In a separate bowl, add 30 drops of the lemon essential oil to the glycerin.

**3**
Mix the glycerin into the dry ingredients.

**4**
Pour the mix into the cellophane bag and tie the bag closed at the top. Store the mix in the paint can.

**5**
Cut one sheet of paper to fit around the outside of the can. Adhere the paper to the can with rubber cement.

**6**
Cut the second sheet of paper so that it is 3 inches shorter than the height of the can. Center it, and rubber cement it to the can.

**7**
Attach the daisies to the can with hot glue.

# Rosy Glow After-Shower Spray

Rose water and glycerin are known for helping to heal super-dry skin. Just spritz this spray on after your shower for shimmery skin and a soft fragrance.

## You Will Need

Measuring cup
½ cup rose water
¼ cup glycerin
Funnel
Medium-size bottle with spray top.
5 drops rose essential oil or 10 drops rose fragrance oil
1 drop red soap color

### 1
Funnel the glycerin and rose water into a spray bottle.

### 2
Add the rose oil and the red color. Replace the spray top, and shake.

### 3
Decorate the container with labels and/or beaded embellishments.

# Herbal Soap

Many herbs have cleansing qualities, and as a bonus they smell great! Try making this simple soap with the herb of your choice. Since the herbs will provide fragrance, you only need to use essential or fragrance oils if you really want a strong smell.

1
Melt the glycerin soap in the microwave.

2
Add yellow color, and stir very gently to distribute it.

3
Add about 2 tablespoons of lemongrass or another herb to the mix, depending on the size of your soap mold. If you want a strong scent, add essential or fragrance oils until you get the smell you want.

4
Pour the mixture slowly into the mold.

5
Let cool and harden completely, and then pop the soap out of the mold.

## Note

*The amount of glycerin soap you'll need depends on the size of your mold. To figure out how much you'll need, pour water into your mold, then pour it into a measuring cup. The amount of water you needed to fill your mold is the same amount of melted soap you'll need.*

## You Will Need

Measuring cup
Grated glycerin soap
Microwave-safe container
Microwave
Stirring implement
10 drops yellow soap color
Dried lemongrass, chamomile, or other herbs
Chamomile, lemongrass, ginger, lavender, or eucalyptus essential or fragrance oils (optional)
Oval-shape mold

# Shapable Soap Sculptures

Making your own soap is a really fun project to do, especially with friends. Try this recipe for moldable soap (a soap you can make into a shape). These soaps look so cool you may not want them to melt away in the shower!

## You Will Need

Measuring cup

Measuring spoons

Small glass bowl

2 tablespoons glycerin

1 heaping tablespoon cornstarch
(plus a little extra)

Soap fragrance of choice

Soap coloring of choice

Wax paper

½-cup clear or opaque glycerin
soap

Knife and cutting board

Microwave

Cellophane wrapping

### 1
In the small glass bowl, mix together the glycerin, cornstarch, and soap color and fragrance.

### 2
Sprinkle a sheet of wax paper with some more cornstarch. Set it aside.

### 3
Cut the soap into cubes and melt it in the microwave. Add color and stir. Pour it into the glass bowl with the cornstarch mix.

### 4
Stir the melted soap into the cornstarch mixture. When the soap starts to harden, pick it up and place it on the sheet of wax paper.

### 5
Coat your hands with cornstarch, and knead the soap until its smooth.

### 6
Mold and remold the soap into the shapes you want, and let them dry on the wax paper. When they're dry, wrap them in cellophane to preserve them.

# Bubbling Bath Bombs

Making these bath bombs is a little bit like a chemistry experiment, but a lot more
fun. Mix up the ingredients, plop them in the tub, and watch them fizz, zing, and
bubble. Bath bombs make great gifts, but keep them away from curious pets or
baby brothers who think they look like candy.

## You Will Need

Glass measuring cup

Measuring spoons

4 or 5 small bowls

¼ cup citric acid

¼ cup cornstarch

¼ cup epsom salts

2 tablespoons borax

½ cup baking soda

Microwave

2 tablespoons coconut oil

Liquid soap colorant

Essential oil of your choice

Wax paper

Soap mold

Cookie sheet

Dish towel

Quart-sized zip-top plastic
sandwich bag

Clear cellophane

Decorative box

### 1
Mix together the citric acid,
cornstarch, epsom salts, borax,
and baking soda in a small bowl,
and set aside.

### 2
Melt the coconut oil in a glass
measuring cup in the microwave
for about 20 seconds or until it is
liquid, but not hot.

### 3
Slowly add the oil to the dry mix.
Add a little bit at a time until the
mixture makes a clump when you
squeeze it in your hand. The mix
will be very dry and crumbly.

### 4
To make the bath bombs
different colors, divide the mixture
into four small bowls before
adding colors and fragrances.

### 5
Add 5 to 10 drops each of the
liquid color and the essential oil to
the coconut oil, and mix.

### 6
Press the mixture firmly into the
molds. Cover the mold with a
piece of wax paper, and then
place a cookie sheet on top.
Carefully flip the whole thing over
so that the cookie sheet is on the
bottom and the mold is on top.

### 7
Carefully remove the mold.

### 8
Cover with a dishtowel, and allow
the bombs to dry and harden for
several days. This is not a great
rainy-day project. The humidity
can cause the bombs to activate.

### 9
Pack the bombs in the zip-top
bag. When you're ready to
present them to a friend, wrap
them in clear cellophane and put
them in a decorative box.

# Rainbow Sherbert Melt and Pour Soap Loaf

Making your own soap is easy, fun, and doesn't cost much. Once you've got the swing of it, you can get creative and try an endless variety of colors, fragrances, and ingredients. Try making this loaf soap first. Once it has set, you can cut it into slices or wedges to use for yourself or give as a gift.

## You Will Need

Grated opaque glycerin soap

Measuring cup

Microwave-safe container

Microwave

Stirring implement

10 drops of soap color in green, pink, and yellow

Soap fragrance of your choice (optional)

Loaf soap mold

Rubbing alcohol and sprayer

Sharp knife or slicer

### Note
*The amount of glycerin soap you'll need depends on the size of your mold. To figure out how much you'll need, pour water into your mold, then pour it into a measuring cup. The amount of water you needed to fill your mold is the same amount of melted soap you'll need.*

**1**
Place the glycerin soap in a microwave-safe container, and melt it in the microwave.

**2**
Stir in a few drops of one color (remember you can always add more, but you can't take it out!). Keep adding color until you get the look you want. When you like the color, stop stirring and pour a somewhat thin layer of soap into the mold. Add fragrance if you like.

**3**
Let this first layer cool and harden. Spray the top of it with rubbing alcohol to prepare it for the next layer to be added.

**4**
Repeats steps 1, 2, and 3 to add a second layer to the loaf mold. Use a different soap color for the second layer.

**5**
Continue adding layers in different colors until you get to the top of the mold. When the last layer has hardened, pop the soap out of the mold, and cut it into wedges or slices.

# Variations

## 1

Try using this same process, but using a different mold. We used a "massage bar" mold to make the small layered soaps. For a smaller mold, you just need to make fewer layers.

## 2

For a different kind of loaf soap, try embedding pieces of one soap inside another. The embedded soap used green soap color and dried eucalyptus leaves, plus eucalyptus soap fragrance. That soap was cut into pieces and used inside an opaque soap.

# Bath Princess Soap Jewels

These sparkly jewels will add fun to your bath and make you feel like a princess. Plus, they're super easy to make!

## You Will Need

Measuring cup

Grated clear glycerin soap

Microwave-safe container

Microwave

Stirring implement

10 drops of soap color in jewel tones

Soap fragrance of your choice (optional)

Jewel-shaped molds

## Note

*The amount of glycerin soap you'll need depends on the size of your mold. To figure out how much you'll need, pour water into your mold, then pour it into a measuring cup. The amount of water you needed to fill your mold is the same amount of melted soap you'll need.*

### 1

Place the grated glycerin soap in a microwave-safe container, and melt it in the microwave.

### 2

Stir in a few drops of one color (remember you can always add more, but you can't take it out!). Keep adding color until you get the look you want. Add fragrance if you want. When you like the color, stop stirring and pour the melted soap into the mold.

### 3

Let the soap cool and harden completely, then pop it out of the mold.

### 4

Repeat the process to create soaps in other colors.

# CHAPTER FOUR

# Body

Think about it: without a healthy body, you couldn't do a lot of the things you like to do. That's why taking care of your body and staying healthy is one of the most important things you can do for yourself. Eating right, exercising, and good grooming are all steps you can take to make sure your body stays in great shape. In this chapter, you'll find body care projects that are fun to make and that help you to look and feel your best. You'll also discover some great tips and advice on body care. Be good to your body and it will be good to you!

# GlitterBug Body Glitter

For a special occasion or just when you're in the mood, spread on a little body glitter for shimmery skin. You decide how much you want to shine by adding a little glitter or a lot. Just remember, you can always add more, but you can't take it away!

### 1
Mix the aloe vera gel, witch hazel, and glycerin in the sandwich bag. Seal the top, and squeeze the bag to mix the contents.

### 2
Add the color one drop at a time until you get the shade you are going for. You may need to add more if you want a darker gel. Add fragrance if you like.

### 3
Add a pinch of glitter, and squeeze again. Add another pinch if you want more shine.

### 4
Snip the tip off of one corner of the bag and gently squeeze the body glitter into one of the bottles.

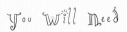

## You Will Need

Measuring spoons
3 tablespoons aloe vera gel
2 tablespoons witch hazel
1 teaspoon glycerin
Zip-top sandwich bag
Scissors
3 to 6 drops liquid soap color
3 to 6 drops soap fragrance
A pinch of shimmery soap glitter
2-ounce clear plastic bottles with squirt tops

## Some fun Combos to try:

Blueberry Blast
*(blue color and berry scent)*

Groovy Grape
*(purple color and berry and apple scent)*

Sour Green Apple
*(green color and apple scent)*

Peachy Keen
*(peach color and peach scent)*

# Your Body:
## THE LONG AND SHORT
## (and Wide and Narrow) of It

When you were younger, you may not have noticed much difference between your body and your best friend's. But starting at about age 10, your hormones, which until then were lying low, start multiplying faster than your pet hamsters! For some girls, it happens early, for others change happens a little later; but eventually you'll start to change too, and it can be a big surprise!

When your hormones kick in, you'll start to see your genes at work. Your genes are like a road map for where your body is going. They've been there since even before you were born, and they start to express themselves a little more strongly as you become a teen. You may sprout and become much taller, or you may fill out and look more like a woman. When all these changes start happening, don't panic! Keeping eating healthy foods and exercising. Your body will go where it's supposed to go naturally. Just relax and try to enjoy discovering the new you!

# Luxury Powder Box

Here's a great gift idea for friends who like a little glamour. This easy-to-make origami box looks beautiful and contains a stash of sparkly powder that's cool to wear on a hot day.

## You Will Need

| | |
|---|---|
| 2 pieces of paper in coordinating patterns, each 12 x 12 inches | Pencil |
| | Measuring cup |
| Ruler | Measuring spoon |
| Clear contact paper | 2 cups cornstarch |
| Scissors | Plastic sandwich bags |
| Craft stick | 1 teaspoon cosmetic grade glitter |
| Hot glue gun and glue sticks | Lavender soap color (powdered) |
| Large white silk flower | Lavender soap scent or essential oil |
| | Powder puff |

## FOR THE POWDER

### 1
Place two cups of cornstarch into one of the plastic bags. Add 1 teaspoon of the glitter and 1/2 teaspoon of the powdered color. Close the bag and shake vigorously to distribute. Add scent a few drops at a time until you are satisfied with the results.

### 2
Transfer the powder to a clean bag. Place in box with powder puff.

## FOR THE BOX

### 1
Trim 1/8 inch from two sides of the piece of paper that you want to use for the box bottom. Make sure that the two sides you cut from are connected at the corner so that the paper remains a square (11 7/8 x 11 7/8).

### 2
Cut two pieces of contact paper that are slightly larger than the paper you wish to cover. Place one piece of paper faceup on a flat surface. Peel back one edge of the contact paper. Place this edge along the edge of the paper. Gently peel the backing off of the contact paper as you smooth it down with your other hand. Rub the contact paper with the edge of the craft stick to make sure that it is firmly attached. Trim edges.

### 3
Fold the four corners of the paper in to the center (see figure 1).

### 4
Crease the paper along the dotted lines (see figure 2).

### 5
Crease again along the dotted lines (see figure 3).

### 6
Open out the top and bottom folds (see figures 4 and 5). Use scissors to cut diagonally in from corners to creased lines.

### 7
Fold up the sides of the paper as shown to form the bottom of the box (see figures 6 and 7).

### 8
Make the lid for the box in the same way, but use a larger piece of paper so that the lid will fit over the box (see figure 8).

### 9
Pull the stem off of the flower, and trim the small plastic nub off of the flower base. Put a small dab of hot glue on the backside of the flower, and press it onto the center of the box top.

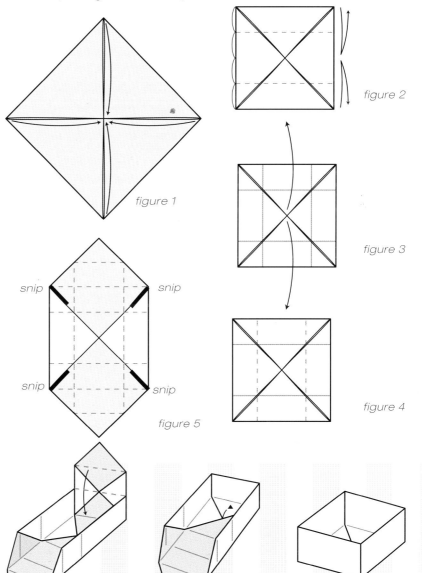

figure 1

figure 2

figure 3

figure 4

snip    snip

snip    snip

figure 5

figure 6

figure 7

figure 8

# Lip Lotion Lip Balm

Your lips can get just as cracked and dry as the rest of your skin, but you can't put moisturizer on them (it doesn't taste so good!). Try making this lip balm to give them the moisture they need. It doesn't leave a sheen like lip gloss—it just sinks right in and gives your lips a soothing soak. This recipe will fill several small tubes, so make a whole batch, fill the containers, then add your fragrance.

## You Will Need

Measuring spoons

Glass measuring cup

3 tablespoons sweet almond oil

¼ cup grated beeswax or beeswax block and grater

1 tablespoon cocoa butter

Microwave

4 vitamin E capsules

Straight pin

Small cup with a pour spout

6 small lip balm tubes

Lip gloss flavoring or candy-making flavoring

Cosmetic-grade powdered soap color (any colors except green and blue)

Cosmetic grade glitter (optional)

Toothpick

### Note

*According to the manufacturer, it's fine to use powdered soap color as coloring for lip gloss. The only two colors that are not safe for use around mucous membranes or your mouth are blue and green. Blue and green powdered colors contain ferric ferrocyanide, a chemical you definitely don't want to get in your mouth.*

# Fruit Punch Lip Gloss

This lip gloss passes the taste test. Unlike a lot of the goopy lip gloss you can get at a store, this one tastes really fresh and rolls on smoothly. Make sure you use essential oil or lip-gloss flavoring—synthetic blends taste like you're eating soap!

**1**
Combine the sweet almond oil, beeswax, and cocoa butter in a small glass measuring cup. Microwave for 30 seconds on high, then check every 20 seconds until the beeswax is completely melted.

**2**
Remove the mixture from heat, and add the vitamin E oil by puncturing the capsules and squirting the contents into the mixture you made in step 1. Stir until thoroughly mixed.

**3**
Carefully pour the mixture into the tubes using the cup with a pour spout.

**4**
Quickly add 3 to 4 drops of flavoring, color, and a pinch of glitter (if you want), and stir with a toothpick.

**5**
Let the balm sit undisturbed until it's solid.

**6**
Repeat the process to fill the remaining containers.

## You Will Need

4 small roll-on glass containers

Straight pin

4 vitamin E capsules

Lip-gloss flavoring or essential oil of your choice

Sweet almond oil

Funnel

**1**
Remove the tops from all four containers.

**2**
Poke a hole in the tip of each vitamin E capsule, and squeeze the contents into each of the bottles.

**3**
Place four drops of flavoring into each of the four bottles.

**4**
Fill the bottles with sweet almond oil.

**5**
Replace the caps and shake.

# Friendly Dragon Breath Spray & Breath Mints

Sometimes you need a quick burst of fresh breath, but there's no time to brush your teeth. For those fresh-breath emergencies, try keeping a stash of homemade breath mints on hand in a little tin you can hide in your pocket or backpack. They also make great gifts!

Spray away bad breath with a quick spritz of this easy-to-make mix. Keep a little spray bottle in your backpack, locker, or gym bag just in case that cheeseburger you had for lunch left your mouth feeling a little less than fresh.

## Spray

### You Will Need

4 ounces distilled water

10 drops peppermint flavoring

4-ounce spray bottle

Place the water and peppermint flavor into the spray bottle, and shake.

## Mints

### You Will Need

Measuring cup

Measuring spoons

Heavy saucepan

Stovetop

Candy thermometer

Small bowl

½ cup corn syrup

½ cup sugar

1 teaspoon peppermint flavor

Confectioner's sugar

Metal tin or small storage container

### 1

Place the corn syrup and sugar in a heavy pan and cook to a hard crack (300° on a candy thermometer). If you don't have a candy thermometer, you can pour a little bit of the mixture into a cup of ice water. The candy is at a hard crack when it solidifies into a ball when it hits the cold water.

### 2

Remove the pan from the heat. Add the peppermint flavor.

### 3

To make the mints, pour ½-teaspoon drops into a small pan that's been coated in confectioner's sugar. Store the mints in a small tin after they've hardened.

# Seven Super Cures for
## Bad Breath

**B**rush your teeth at least twice a day with fluoride toothpaste.

**1**

When you brush your teeth, make sure to give your tongue a brushing as well, because most of the odor-causing bacteria in your mouth live there.

**2**

Drink lots of water to stimulate saliva flow and to rinse away food and bacteria between brushings.

**3**

Avoid foods that are guaranteed to cause bad breath such as cabbage, garlic, and onions. Dairy products can be even worse! They coat your mouth with a layer of lactose, which breaks down into very stinky sulfurous bacteria.

**4**

Make sure to brush afterwards if you do eat these odor-causing foods.

**5**

Most gum problems are the result of rotting food left in the spaces between your teeth.

**6**

Floss your teeth once a day to reduce the risk of gum disease and cavities between teeth, and to keep your breath smelling fresh.

**7**

Get a dental checkup twice a year.

# Just the Facts on Bad Breath

### MYTH

You can smell your own bad breath.

### FACT

You can't tell if you have bad breath because you get used to your own smell.

### MYTH

If you brush your teeth twice a day, you won't have bad breath.

### FACT

Although brushing certainly helps, bad breath can be caused by lots of things other than your last meal. Cavities, sinus problems, or sickness can all make your breath smell a little yucky.

### MYTH

Your tongue is like a piece of pink skin.

### FACT

Your tongue is more like a thick dense carpet. It is warm, moist, thick, and spongy, making it a great place for bacteria to breed.

### MYTH

Bad breath is caused by the food we eat.

### FACT

Bad breath comes from bacteria in your mouth that produces odor-causing sulfur compounds. Because the tongue's surface is spongy and carpet-like, bacteria collect in the cracks and crevices on the back of your tongue.

# Summer Breeze Solid Perfume

You may think making a perfume is some mysterious process that takes place only in professional labs in Paris. Not true! You can make your own solid perfume in your very own kitchen, no white lab coat required.
Just dab it on to use it—the fragrance lasts a long, long time.

## You Will Need

Measuring spoons

3 tablespoons grated beeswax or beeswax block and grater

Double boiler

Small bowl

6 tablespoons sweet almond oil

4 vitamin E capsules

Straight pin

Essential oils or fragrance oils

Small metal tins with lids

**Note**
*You may substitute fragrance oils for essential oils in this recipe. Because soap scents are water based and will not mix with oil, they do not work well in this recipe.*

*This recipe will fill 10 small tins.*

**1**
Combine the grated beeswax and almond oil. Melt the mixture in a double boiler.

**2**
Remove from heat and add the vitamin E oil by puncturing the capsules and squirting the contents into the mixture you made in step 1.

**3**
Fill a small container almost to the top. Add 8 to 10 drops of essential oil or fragrance oil, and stir with a toothpick. Leave the mixture undisturbed until it solidifies.

# Perfumania!

Are you a fragrance fanatic? Even though you may love your kiwi-lime body wash, rose-geranium lotion, and vanilla body spray, don't wear them all at once! People will be able to smell you before they can see you, and too much of a good smell can give the people around you a headache, too. Whether you choose to wear scented oil, lotion, or cologne, less is more.

Fragrances are made up of combinations of many different essential oils that are absorbed into your skin at different rates. How a fragrance smells on you depends mostly on your body chemistry and your diet—the same fragrance can smell very different on different people. Find a signature scent that you really love and use it lightly by spraying it in front of you, then walking through it. Fragrance absorbs into dry skin more quickly than it does into oily skin. If you feel your fragrance fades too fast, make it last longer by layering it with a matching body lotion.

# Good Clean Fun Liquid Hand Soap

Add a fun factor to your hand washing routine!
These soap dispensers look cool in your bathroom
and make great gifts.

## You Will Need

Measuring spoons

Clear liquid soap

2 teaspoons glycerin

Zip-top sandwich bag

A few drops liquid soap color

A few drops soap fragrance

A pinch of cosmetic grade glitter

Embeds (metallic glitter, dice, small plastic figures, etc.)

Scissors

8-ounce clear plastic bottles with pump dispenser tops

### 1
Mix the soap and glycerin in the sandwich bag.

### 2
Add color, fragrance, and/or glitter to the mix until you get the look you want. Add one drop at a time. If the color gets too dark you won't be able to see the embeds.

### 3
Place the embeds into the bottle.

### 4
Snip a corner off of the bag, and squeeze the contents into the bottle.

### 5
As a variation, skip the embeds and use color and glitter to embellish the soap.

# The Girl-on-the-Go Bag

A girl on the go needs a bag to go with her. Whether you're going on a quick trip to the gym, a family vacation, or to an overnight slumber party, keep all your bath and beauty supplies in one bag that's ready to go when you are. When you finish soccer practice and have to go straight to a party, you'll have your travel kit ready, so you can transform from soccer star into dancing queen at a moment's notice. To stock your bag, start with travel sizes of items that you use everyday:

- Shampoo
- Conditioner
- Toothbrush in a case
- Toothpaste
- Dental floss
- Lip balm
- Liquid soap (bar soap tends to get gummy and gross looking)
- Deodorant (if you use it)
- Lotion
- Hair brush or comb

**Note:**
*If you wear glasses or a retainer and have an extra pair, keep it in the bag for emergencies, too!*

# The Dirt on Sweat...

As you get closer to becoming a teenager, your body starts producing more and more hormones. Hormones create a lot of changes, one of which is more perspiration. Perspiration or sweating happens when your body tries to control its temperature by releasing water and salts. Sweat itself doesn't cause an odor; that happens when the bacteria on your skin (we all have it!) mixes with sweat.

There are other factors that can cause your body odor to be stronger. Diet is part of it (eating strong-smelling foods with lots of garlic and onions for example), but your body may also create more odor if it has an infection.

*Hormones Create a lot of Changes*

Certain drugs, herbs, alcohol, and cigarette smoke can also cause body odor.

Keeping clean can help you avoid body odor. As you enter your teen years, you might find that you need to bathe or shower more often. Depending on what you eat, your body chemistry, and how much you exercise, you may need to make a daily effort to wash those particularly odor-prone areas like underarms.

At a certain point, you may consider using a product to combat body odors. Here's a list of the products out there and what they do.

Crystal deodorant stones are made from crystallized potassium sulfate. Potassium sulfate slows the growth of odor-causing bacteria on your body. Because deodorant crystals come from a natural mineral, they are perfectly natural, and because they are so gentle, they are generally the best place to start when you first feel you might need a deodorant. To use a deodorant crystal, gently rub the crystal under your arms while they're still wet. The crystal will last a very long time if it's used correctly. Rinse and dry the crystal after using it. Store it in a dry place, and be careful not to drop it. Occasionally small scratchy crystals may form around the edges if the crystal is exposed to moisture.

# and Smells

If this occurs, rinse the crystal with warm water and dry it thoroughly.

Antiperspirants suppress perspiration. This keeps you from getting wet spots under your arms if you're prone to this sort of thing.

Deodorants kill the smell. Make sure your underarms are clean and dry before applying deodorant. Sometimes even with deodorant, some people have a problem with body odor. If you feel that you might fall into this category, try this for a few days: wipe your underarms with a cotton ball soaked in white vinegar before you shower.

## Sweat is Beautiful!

Keeping fit and getting exercise not only makes you feel better, it actually makes you look better too: your skin glows because your blood is circulating, and you're getting a good workout. Even if you're not the Olympic-athlete type, get moving, doing whatever it is you like to do. Ride a bike, go for a walk and look at wildflowers, swim at the pool, or dance up a storm. Team sports are great too, and as an added benefit, they can lead to great friendships! Leave your computer behind for a while, and try some physical activity—you'll be really glad you did.

# CHAPTER FIVE

# Hands & Feet

Have you ever heard the expression "put your best foot forward"? It means to make a good first impression. Hands and feet are really out there in the spotlight getting noticed. When you meet someone new, you shake hands, and if it's summer and you're wearing sandals, everyone gets a good look at your toes. But all that exposure means hands and feet get extra roughed up. This chapter focuses on taking care of these important body parts and helping them recover from all the wear and tear they experience every day. You'll also learn how to dress them up with manicures, pedicures, nail art, and cool accessories.

# Just Rosy Hand Cream

You use your hands for just about everything from sports to crafts to doing your homework. All that hard work can leave them feeling chapped and rough. This rose hand cream heals tired, overworked hands instantly, and, as an added bonus, it makes them smell just rosy!

## You Will Need

Glass measuring cup

Measuring spoons

¼ cup rose water

¼ cup glycerin

½ cup aloe vera gel

½ teaspoon borax

Blender or hand-mixer and bowl

½ cup grapeseed oil

2 tablespoons cocoa butter

⅓ cup beeswax chips or beeswax block and grater

1 teaspoon lanolin

4 drops rose soap fragrance

4 drops red soap color

2 glass or plastic jars, each 4 ounces

## Hand Cream

### 1

Combine the rose water, glycerin, aloe vera gel, and borax in a blender or small bowl, and blend until the gel has liquefied and the borax has dissolved.

### 2

Combine the grapeseed oil, cocoa butter, beeswax, and lanolin in a small glass measuring cup. Microwave for 30 seconds on high, then check every 20 seconds' until the beeswax and lanolin are completely melted.

### 3

Start your blender. Slowly drizzle the oil mixture into the aloe mix. Go slowly—if you pour too fast, the ingredients will separate instead of blend. Mix really well, until the two mixtures have emulsified (see page 13) and look like mayonnaise

# Rose-So-Soft Cuticle Softener

You may never think about your cuticles (that border of skin around your nails) until they start to hurt. Every once in a while, that soft skin can get torn, and your fingers can start to feel rough and painful. If it happens to you, don't pull at the skin—that will only make it worse. Try this soothing potion that helps your skin heal in a hurry.

## You Will Need

Small glass bottle with an eyedropper top

Measuring spoons

2 tablespoons sweet almond oil

Funnel

4 drops rose essential oil (or rose fragrance oil)

Straight pin

3 vitamin E capsules

Water

Teakettle or saucepan

Stovetop

Tea or coffee cup

**5**

Warm the oil by placing the bottle in a cup of hot water, then apply a drop to each nail.

**6**

After a few minutes, use your fingers to gently push your cuticles back. Rub the remaining oil into your nails for a soft, natural sheen.

## Cuticle Softener

**1**

Pour the sweet almond oil into the bottle using the funnel.

**2**

Add the essential oil.

**3**

Poke a hole into the end of the vitamin E capsules, and squeeze the oil into the bottle.

**4**

Put the top on the bottle, and shake.

**4**

Add fragrance and color. Pour the mixture into the jars while it's warm. It will set quickly as it cools.

# Mad About Mendhi

Mendhi is the ancient art of creating beautiful exotic tattoos with henna paste. The tradition of mendhi comes from North Africa and the Middle East and has been around for over 5,000 years. You can copy the templates we provide or come up with some simple patterns of your own. This batch is large enough for you and several friends to enjoy.

## You Will Need

¼ cup henna powder

Glass bowls

Spoon

2 lemons

Very strong hot coffee

Cellophane

Plastic bottle with mist top or squirt bottle

Templates on page 123

Flat toothpicks

Small paintbrushes

Zip-top plastic sandwich bag

Scissors

Vegetable oil

Petroleum jelly (optional)

### Note

*It takes 2 to 4 weeks for mendhi to wear off. Warning! Beware of people offering black henna tattoos. They are not really made with henna, but with P-phenylenediamine, a toxic black chemical dye that can cause skin blisters and liver damage!*

**1**
Place the henna in a glass bowl.

**2**
Add the juice of one lemon and stir until the henna makes a very thick paste.

**3**
Stir in the hot coffee just a little at a time until the paste is smooth, not so thick, and not runny! Cover with cellophane and refrigerate for one day.

## To Apply

**1**
Juice the second lemon, strain it (remove the seeds), and pour the contents into a small mister bottle.

**2**
Wash your skin so that all your lotion is removed. Dry thoroughly.

**3**
Apply the mendhi with flat toothpicks, or you can paint it on with a paintbrush if you thin

it with some more lemon juice first. Another technique is to put the mendhi into a small sandwich bag. Snip a tiny hole off one corner and apply the henna by squirting it out like you are decorating a cake or use a small bottle with a little applicator tip. Henna will stain your clothes and anything else it touches, so watch out!

### 4

Keep the mendhi moist on your skin for 4 to 5 hours by misting it with lemon juice. The longer you leave the henna on your skin, the darker the stain will become.

### 5

If you want to let it develop overnight, carefully wrap the design in toilet paper, spritz it with a little lemon juice, then wrap it in plastic wrap.

### 6

The design will last longer if you remove the henna by rubbing it with a little vegetable oil. It will also last longer if you put petroleum jelly on it before bathing, showering, or getting in the pool.

# Tattoo You!

Your parents would definitely say "no way!" if you asked for a real tattoo, but these fun temporary tattoos let your play around and express yourself without doing permanent damage! They're made from special non-toxic tattoo gel pens (make sure to use only non-toxic ones). Test the gel pen on a small spot on your arm and let it sit for a few hours to make sure that you are not allergic. These tattoos only last a few days, but if you really need to get your latest work of art off before your family photo or visit with Grandma, a hard scrub with rubbing alcohol ought to do it!

# Fancy Fingers Nail Design

You don't need a bunch of store-bought decals to make your nails look cool. Paint your own designs using cotton swabs and toothpicks. You'll save money, and your nails will be unique,

## You Will Need

Nail polish in lots of colors
Nail polish remover
Cotton swabs
Cotton balls
Toothpicks

### 1
Use your imagination, and get creative with different patterns and designs.

### 2
Snap the tip off of a cotton swab and use it to make polka dots.

### 3
Add small details with toothpicks.

## Hand and Nail Tips

If your nails look a little yellow, try soaking them in a little water and fresh lemon juice. Rub your nails with the lemon, and put your hands back into the juice. The juice will bleach your nails and remove any stains.

Tired of that dry skin on your hands and feet? Mix 3 tablespoons of sweet almond oil with 3 tablespoons of ground almonds to make a quick scrub that will remove all of it. Gently rub for a few minutes, then rinse and pat dry. Voila!

Buff your nails with almond oil for a natural nail polish.

# Manicure Basics

Taking care of your nails doesn't have to be a chore—it can actually be fun. Once you've got these basics down, nail care will become so easy you could do it while talking on the phone or even doing your homework (just kidding!).

Start by removing any polish with nail polish remover.

File nails in one direction with an emery board. Going back and forth damages the nail.

Shape the nail to suit your style. Some people like ovals, others like their nails straight across. You decide! Try to avoid filing the sides, because this weakens the nail. Rinse and dry your hands to remove dust.

Apply a drop of cuticle softener to the base of each nail, and let it sit for a few minutes.

For a special treatment, warm the cuticle softener in a bowl of hot water while you're filing. Gently rub the softener in and push your cuticles back.

Buff your nails with a soft cloth. They'll have a nice natural shine.

Massage lotion into your hands.

Every now and then it's fun to put a coat of polish on for special occasions. When you want to take the next step, make sure that your nails are lotion free by rubbing them with a little alcohol on a cotton ball.

Dip your brush into the polish, grabbing just enough to cover one nail at a time. Carefully paint the nail with a few small strokes. Use several thin coats rather than one big glob (you won't get as many smudges that way).

Now sit still and let the polish dry!

# Footcare Line

## Winter Mint Crystals Footbath

Epsom salts and sea salt combined with natural oils make a wonderfully soothing footbath. After all your feet have done for you today, don't they deserve a treat?

### 1
Separate 1½ cups of the sea salt in a separate bowl.

### 2
Mix the remaining dry ingredients in a bowl.

### 3
Add the oils one at a time, stirring between additions.

### 4
Color the mixture with the blue and green dye soap color, stirring well between each addition.

### 5
Divide the remaining salt in half in two separate bowls. Color one bowl of salt green and the other blue, adding a few drops at a time until you get the look you want.

### 6
Mix everything together.

### 7
Pour the mixture into the cellophane bag, then store the bag in a metal can. Decorate the can with labels or other embellishments.

### You Will Need
Measuring cup

Small bowls

2 ½ cups sea salt

1 cup epsom salts

½ cup baking soda

¼ cup borax

Spoon

10 drops peppermint oil

10 drops tea tree oil

10 drops eucalyptus oil

Blue soap color

Green soap color

Cellophane bag

1-quart unused paint can

# Snow Faerie Foot Dust

Looking for a quick fix for tired, smelly feet? Rub some of this soothing powder on them, and they'll be good as new.

## You Will Need

Measuring cup

Measuring spoons

Small bowl

Large metal powder shaker

½ cup baking soda

½ cup cornstarch

2 tablespoons bentonite clay

10 drops peppermint oil

10 drops eucalyptus oil

10 drops tea tree oil

Blue powdered soap color

Wire whisk

Funnel

**1**
Mix all dry ingredients in a small bowl.

**2**
Add the oils one at a time, whisking after each addition.

**3**
Funnel the powder into the container.

# Misty Day Foot Spray

As you probably already know, feet are one of those parts of the body that can start to smell after a good workout (or even if they've been stuffed in a pair of shoes on a hot day). Try this refreshing spray to eliminate the odor—it's like perfume especially for your feet!

## You Will Need

Funnel

4-ounce pump spray bottle

Measuring cup

2 ounces witch hazel

1 ounce distilled water

Peppermint essential oil

Eucalyptus essential oil

Tea tree oil

Rubbing alcohol

**1**
Use the funnel to pour the witch hazel into the bottle.

**2**
Add 10 drops each of the peppermint, tea tree, and eucalyptus oils.

**3**
Top off the bottle with the rubbing alcohol.

**4**
Replace the spray top.

**5**
Shake before using.

# Gypsy Girl Toe Rings

Dress them up or dress them down with the variety of buttons available, the possibilities for fanciful foot self-expression are limitless!

## 1
Cut a 6-inch piece of elastic.

## 2
Thread 10 glass beads onto the elastic.

## 3
Thread the elastic through to the top of a button; add two more beads, then thread it back through to the backside of the button.

## 4
Measure the toe ring size by wrapping it around your toe. It should be tight enough to stay on without flopping around, but you don't want it to cut off circulation!

## 5
Add a few more beads, if necessary. Thread both ends of the elastic through a crimp bead, double-check the size, and then press a crimp bead with the pliers to flatten it.

## 6
Trim the excess cord.

## You Will Need

Scissors

Ruler or measuring tape

Clear stretching beading elastic

Small glass beads

Collection of small buttons

Crimp beads

Pliers

# The Manicure/Pedicure Everything Kit

**W**hen you've got a nail emergency, you don't want to waste time rummaging through the bathroom cabinet to find your nail file or clippers. Keep everything together in one place so you can fix your nails in a flash. Find a cute zip-up bag that's small enough to carry with you. Here's a list of things you should keep in your kit:

- Orange sticks
- Pumice stone
- Fingernail clippers
- Toenail clippers

- Nailbrush
- Nail file
- Clear polish
- Cuticle oil

# Pedicure Basics

You don't need to go to a salon for a first-rate pedicure. You can give yourself one at home, and your toes will look just as great. Follow the instructions below, and you'll be a pro in no time. Once you've got the hang of it, throw a pedicure party with your friends so you can all practice on each other.

● Remove all polish.

● Trim your toenails straight across. Do not trim the sides—it causes ingrown toenails.

● File your nails in one direction to prevent damage to the nail.

● Put a drop or two of cuticle oil onto the base of each toenail.

● Soak your feet in a small shallow pan of warm water for a few minutes.

● Throw a handful of foot salts or marbles into the tub for a little extra treat.

● Dry your feet, and gently push back your cuticles with an orange stick. This should not be painful!

● Massage your feet with lotion.

● Wipe your toenails with a cotton ball soaked in alcohol to remove all residue before painting.

● At this point you have three options: rub your toenails with a little oil (cuticle oil works fine) for a natural shine, paint them with the solid color of your choice, or get creative and make those toes a true statement of your individuality!

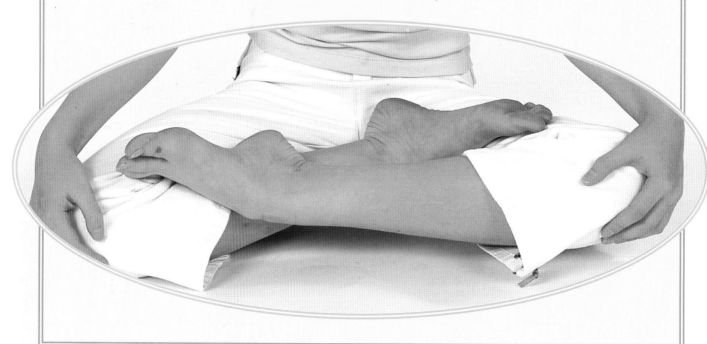

# Is That My Feet?

## Foot Odor and What to Do About It

Being the active girl you are, you may find that when you take off your shoes, you're faced with an unpleasant smell. Could that possibly be your feet? You're not the first one to face that surprise, so here's some advice from those who have been there before.

● Make sure you wash your feet with soap and water every day.

● Make sure to dry your feet thoroughly.

● Always wear socks with closed-toed shoes.

● Change your socks every day (keep an extra pair in your gym bag).

● If at all possible, have separate pairs of shoes: save one pair especially for sports and exercise. By doing this, you can change out of your hot, sweaty shoes after practice and give them a chance to air out.

● If you've tried all of the above and still have a problem, try this for a few days in a row: before bathing, wipe off your feet with a cotton ball soaked in white vinegar.

● A lightly scented odor-absorbing powder can also be helpful if you don't have the time to shower after exercising or sports activities.

Take care of your feet – one step at a time

# CHAPTER SIX

# Mind and Spirit

Your health isn't just about your body. What you feel on the inside can really affect how your body functions and how healthy you feel on the outside. If you get too stressed, you may notice that you start to feel low energy and get sick more often. Making sure you feel calm and relaxed on the inside is really important, but it can sometimes be hard to do. With all your activities and responsibilities, you may feel a little overwhelmed. Try making the projects and using some of the techniques in this chapter to slow down a little, relax, and enjoy yourself.

# Relaxation Techniques

id you know that relaxation can be learned just like any other skill, like dancing or playing soccer? Try these tips below for a mellower you:

● Close your eyes and take 10 deep breaths. Inhale slowly through your nose, and exhale slowly through your mouth. Ahhh…now isn't that better?

● Squeeze the muscles in your whole body, and hold them in as long as you can. Now shake them out, and let the tension go.

● Warm water is one of the greatest luxuries in the world. Take a nice, long, warm soak. It'll cure almost anything!

● Lie down on a small rug or folded blanket, and stretch a little. Think about getting a book on yoga and practicing some postures. It feels great!

● Exercise is a great way to take away that extra stress. Plus, when you exercise it causes your body to release endorphins, a natural chemical that makes you feel fantastic!

● Journaling is a great way to vent the frustrations of the day. Record your thoughts and dreams. It helps you get in touch with your goals, and later you can look back to see how far you have come!

● Music can be very soothing when you're really stressed out. Pick some mellow music out of your collection, turn it on low, and chill.

● Express your creativity by doing crafts, writing poetry, or practicing some dance moves. Don't censor yourself or let anyone else judge your work. The goal is to loosen up and have fun. And you have to start somewhere.

● Laugh it off! Call your best friend, and tell her all the details. She's sure to make you laugh about it.

# Sweet Dreams Eye Pillow

After a tough day, instead of plopping in front of the TV, trying going to an empty room, closing your eyes, and pressing on this lavender eye pillow. Lavender is the ultimate relaxing herb and will give you instant relief. After just a few minutes, you'll feel your stress melt away, and you'll be ready to tackle your homework!

**1**

Cut out two 4 x 9-inch rectangles of fabric.

**2**

Cut two 3 ½-inch pieces of beaded fringe.

**3**

Place one piece of fabric right side up on a flat surface. Center one piece of fringe on each end of the fabric. The fringe should be pointing toward the center of the fabric, and the ribbon edge should be lined up with the edge of the fabric. Place the second piece of fabric facedown on top of the fringe, and pin in place.

**4**

Sew the two pieces of fabric together, leaving a ½-inch seam allowance. Leave a 2-inch opening for the stuffing.

**5**

Turn the pillow right side out. Fill it with lavender and rice. Stitch the opening closed.

## You Will Need

Measuring tape

Scissors

¼ yard of soft fabric

Coordinated beaded ribbon fringe

Straight pins

Sewing machine

Dried lavender

Rice

Needle

Thread

# Rites of Passage

It's important to celebrate your accomplishments and mark changes and transitions in your life. Around the world, some cultures mark the transition to adulthood with rites of passage. Adolescence in these cultures isn't really recognized—one day you are a child, and the next you become an adult. Consider exploring your heritage with your parents and coming up with your own rite of passage to mark special events in your life.

An Apache girls' puberty ceremony lasts for four days and includes storytelling and an elaborate feast. The ceremony is supposed to make her generous, kind, and strong.

The rite of passage ceremonies of Australian Aborigines include ritual bathing and separation from the tribe for periods of time. Traditionally, a girl gets married and goes to live with her husband's family as soon as she hits puberty.

A quinceanera is a special ceremony for 15-year-old girls of Spanish descent. Every May, a special candlelit Catholic mass is held for all fifteen-year-old girls. Each girl chooses 14 of her best girlfriends (one for each year of her life) to be her honored guests. Afterwards, there is a party where the birthday girl dances a waltz with her father, and then with whomever else she chooses.

Jewish girls celebrate their 13th birthday with a bat mitzvah, during which the young girl recites a portion of the Torah, then enjoys a big party.

# Bouquet Sachets

For a little lift every time you open your dresser drawers, try making these fragrant sachets. Their wonderful smell will stick to your clothes and give you a fresh feeling all day. They also make great gifts!

**1**
Following the manufacturer's instructions, iron on the embellishments to the fabric pouches. You may need to use a press cloth if the fabric is delicate.

**2**
Place 2 to 3 tablespoons of herbs into the center of each muslin rectangle. Fold the edges in to make a small packet of herbs.

**3**
Place the herb-filled fabric squares into the fabric pouches.

**4**
Pull the drawstring to close the opening, and tie it in a tight bow.

## You Will Need

Small fabric pouches with drawstring closures

Iron-on embellishments

Iron and ironing board

Press cloth

White muslin fabric cut into 4 x 6-inch squares

Assortment of dried herbs (such as lemongrass, lavender, and cedar)

Measuring spoon

Measuring bowl

# Zen Sand Garden

Have you heard of a Zen garden? It's a Japanese traditional garden that includes raking patterns into sand. This kind of garden is meant to inspire meditation and contemplation (that means deep thinking). If you need a calming focus point in your room, try this simple sand garden. Stare at it when you've got a tough homework problem, and maybe you'll have a breakthrough!

## You Will Need

Clear, flat, decorative glass pebbles

Paper towels

Rubbing alcohol

Paintbrushes

Glass paint pens

Glass paint

Clear acrylic sealer

Small tray

Colored sand

Small comb

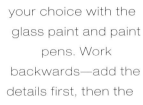

## 1
Wipe off the glass pebbles with the rubbing alcohol.

## 2
Paint the underside of the glass pebbles in the pattern of your choice with the glass paint and paint pens. Work backwards—add the details first, then the background. The pattern possibilities are endless! Allow drying time.

## 3
Paint the pebbles with clear sealer.

## 4
Pour the colored sand into the tray.

## 5
Use the comb to create patterns in the sand, and then artfully display your painted pebbles!

# Stress Busters

We all have those days. Too much homework, didn't make the team, annoying younger siblings getting on your nerves. Sometimes everything happens all at once. Even if you're having lots of fun, you can get stressed out by overextending yourself. When you feel maxed out, it's especially important take care of yourself. Plan on doing something for yourself the next time you get stressed. Taking time off to do the things you really love, even if it's just for a few minutes, can leave you relaxed, recharged, and ready to go again!

# You're Never Too Old for Teddy

## HOT PAD

Just because you're grown up doesn't mean you don't need a teddy bear anymore. This one has a special feature: he's filled with a fragrant blend of relaxing herbs to soothe your aching muscles after you've overdone it on the playing field or at the gym. Just heat him in the microwave for two to three minutes and snuggle up.

## You Will Need

Template on page 123

½ yard of dark cotton chenille or a hand towel

Measuring tape or ruler

Scissors

2 non-metallic buttons

Thread

Needle

Sewing machine or patience to hand sew

Wooden spoon

Measuring cup

2 cups flax or rice

½ cup dried peppermint leaves

½ cup dried bergamot

Mixing bowl

Funnel

1 yard of ribbon (not the wired kind)

Fray check or clear nail polish

### 1
Fold the fabric in half with right sides together. Photocopy and cut out the template pattern, and place it on top of the fabric. Cut the fabric around the pattern.

### 2
Position the two buttons on the face area of the bear, placing them where you want the eyes to be. Sew them onto the right side of the fabric.

### 3
Use the needle and thread and the template on page 123 to embroider the nose and mouth onto the teddy's face.

### 4
Place the fabric pieces together with right sides facing. Sew around the edges of the fabric leaving a ½-inch seam allowance. Leave a 2-inch opening so you'll be able to fill the teddy.

### 5
Snip the seams at the corners so your bear won't be bulky. Turn the bear right side out. Use the end of a wooden spoon to push out the arms and legs.

### 6
Mix the peppermint, bergamot, and flax or rice in a small bowl.

### 7
Funnel the mix into the bear. Whipstitch the opening closed (see figure 1).

### 8
Tie the ribbon around the teddy's neck. Trim the ends of the ribbon by folding them in half and cutting up diagonally toward the crease. Treat the ends with fray check or clear nail polish.

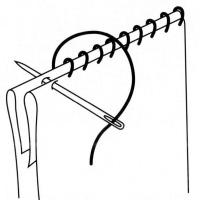

*Figure 1*

# Aromatherapy Room Sprays

If your dull, drab room is getting you down, you don't need to redecorate. Try adding a fresh scent to give it a makeover. An aromatherapy spray can make a room seem happier instantly and might be just what you need to lift your spirits.

### 1
Funnel 1 tablespoon of rubbing alcohol into each spray bottle.

### 2
Add the grapefruit essential oil and peach soap color to one bottle, then fill up the rest of the bottle with the distilled water.

### 3
Add the lavender essential oil and lilac soap color to the second bottle, then fill up the rest of the bottle with the distilled water.

### 4
Shake before using.

## You Will Need

2 spray bottles, each 4-ounces

Funnel

Measuring spoons

2 tablespoons rubbing alcohol

10 drops grapefruit essential oil (or 15 drops of fragrance oil)

1 drop peach soap color

Distilled water

10 drops lavender essential oil (or 15 drops of fragrance oil)

2 drops lilac soap color

# MENDHI, TATTOO AND TEDDY BEAR TEMPLATES

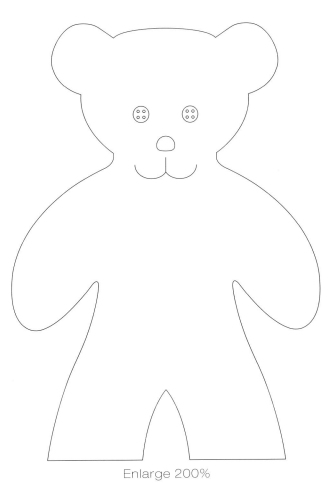

Enlarge 200%

# LABEL TEMPLATES

## ACKNOWLEDGMENTS

There are many people who I would like to acknowledge who were incredibly supportive during the writing of this book. I'm so blessed to have had the opportunity to work with a group of extremely talented and creative people. Thanks to Joanne O'Sullivan, my wonderfully talented and patient editor, for sharing her wisdom and encouragement, and for sharing her way with words. Thanks to my fabulously gifted and inspired art director Dana Irwin for all of her work in the design of this book and the labels. Thanks to children's book editor Joe Rhatigan for his encouragement. Thanks also to Deborah Morgenthal for her friendship, faith, and encouragement, and for giving me a chance. You're the best!

I would also like to acknowledge my mother, father, and step-mom, Kathy. Thanks for your love, and unfailing support and encouragement. Special thanks to my dear friend Claire Payne, the charter member of my fan club. Marta Acala-Williams was a big help with the hair care section and a great friend—thanks so much. Thanks to my mother-in-law, Donia, for sharing with me her deep appreciation for art and beauty in life. I also wish to thank my honorary triplets, Craig and Crandall, the masters of good grooming. To Kathy Sheldon, Silvia Swiger, Gloria Good, and JoAnne Comito, the members of my Artists Way group—Thanks! It worked! Thanks also to my brother Parker who is a living example that it is possible to make a living doing something you truly love. Most importantly, thanks to my husband, Tama, for being such a tremendous source of unfailing support, encouragement, and unconditional love. I love you all so much!

Several companies generously donated many of the products used in the book. Special thanks to:

**Life of the Party, Sunburst Bottle Company, Spice of Life**

The inspiring wallpaper samples seen in the photos are from the Watercolors Collection by Waverly, a Division of F. Schumacher & Co., 79 Madison Ave., New York, NY 10016, www.decoratewaverly.com.

Usually, the supplies you need for making the projects in Lark books can be found at your local craft supply store, discount mart, home improvement center, or retail shop relevant to the topic of the book. Occasionally, however, you may need to buy materials or tools from specialty suppliers. In order to provide you with the most up-to-date information, we have created suppliers listings on our Web site, which we update on a regular basis. Visit us at www.larkbooks.com, click on "Craft Supply Sources," and then click on the relevant topic. You will find numerous companies listed with their web address and/or mailing address and phone number.

Finally, the book would not look as great as it does without the help of our talented models. Thanks to:

Monique Bowie

Sarah Comito

Anna Comito

Daniela Diaz

Devon Dickerson

Anna Weshner Dunning

Hana Harper

Lauren Lien

Corrina Matthews

India Good-Prochaska

Emily Samsel

Leila Scoggin

Erika Swiger

Isabel Williams

Chelsea Wise

## METRIC CONVERSION TABLE

| INCHES | CENTIMETERS |
| --- | --- |
| 1/8 | 3 mm |
| 1/4 | 6 mm |
| 3/8 | 9 mm |
| 1/2 | 1.3 |
| 5/8 | 1.6 |
| 3/4 | 1.9 |
| 7/8 | 2.2 |
| 1 | 2.5 |
| 1 1/4 | 3.1 |
| 1 1/2 | 3.8 |
| 1 3/4 | 4.4 |
| 2 | 5 |
| 2 1/2 | 6.25 |
| 3 | 7.5 |
| 3 1/2 | 8.8 |
| 4 | 10 |
| 4 1/2 | 11.3 |
| 5 | 12.5 |
| 5 1/2 | 13.8 |
| 6 | 15 |
| 7 | 17.5 |
| 8 | 20 |
| 9 | 22.5 |
| 10 | 25 |
| 11 | 27.5 |
| 12 | 30 |

Our
Models

DEVON

SARAH

ERIKA

HANA

INDIA

CORRINA

ISABEL

MONIQUE

LEILA

CHELSEA

DANIELA

ANNA

LAUREN

EMILY

ANNA

# Index

ALLISON CHANDLER SMITH lives in Asheville, North Carolina. In addition to operating an interior redesign business, she works as a freelance crafter and designer. Her designs have appeared in numerous Lark books, including *Summer Style, Decorating Baskets, Girls' World, Kids' Crafts: Soapmaking,* and *Decorating Candles.* For more information, visit lemondropdesign.com.